ENDORSEMENTS

Before you and your partner get bogged down in decision-making about seating charts and cutlery choices, you need to read this book. It will help you make a decision about your name that will last long after the honeymoon has ended.

–Talia Burkett - Wedding Photographer, Sister B Studios

Marcia's book is an incredible, comprehensive guide that helps modern couples process the options, protocols, and procedures regarding changing their names after marriage. She outlines the historical symbolization and contemporary considerations for merging a couple's personal identities, cultural backgrounds, individual personalities, career achievements, and social branding.

–Trish Jones - Wedding Designer & Planner, The Walk Down the Aisle

Should I Change My Name? gave me the tools to decide what to do about my own name. The book unwraps the complex traditions and history of married last names and is a great read for newlyweds!

–Morgan McCollum - Bride

This book is a fascinating journey into the psychology of naming. Every couple will grow closer by reading it together.

–Philip Kenney - Marriage and Family Therapist

I wish this book had been around when I was married!

–Rev. Carrie Finegan - Wedding Officiant

Should I Change My Name? sets out clearly the reasons for and against every surname choice you might be thinking of making.

–Richard Coates, Ph.D. - Professor Emeritus of Onomastics, Bristol Centre for Linguistics, University of the West of England

I love recommending this book to our couples! It helps them thoughtfully decide on the name that feels right for them.

–Bree Denman - Wedding Planner, The Indigo Bride

Conflicted about changing your surname when you marry? In *Should I Change My Name?*, Morgan offers a helpful round-the-world history on naming and sound tips to help you decide.

–Ann Simas - Romance Writer and Author of Disappearing Act

If only I'd had this book as I planned a wedding, career, and family - a great read and resource.

–Susan Cooper - Attorney and Mediator

Should I Change My Name? is a must-read for anyone getting married or for those simply interested in last name decisions at the time of marriage. In addition to the history of marital naming and naming practices across countries, the book includes detailed information on each type of marital naming choice and the benefits and challenges of each choice. This information, along with excerpts from individuals having made each of the six naming choices, provides those considering their marital naming options details about thoughts and experiences of others, which can help readers make an informed decision for themselves. The chapter focusing on talking with a partner about marital naming can help a couple making a name choice that fits the needs of both partners. There are no right or wrong surname choices at the time of marriage and this book provides people with the information to make the decision that best serves the needs of each partner. *Should I Change My Name?* is a one-stop information source for couples thinking about last name decisions at the time of marriage.

–Laurie Scheuble, Ph.D. - Professor Emeritus of Sociology, Pennsylvania State University

SHOULD I CHANGE MY NAME?

The Impact of
Your Last Name on Identity,
Marriage, and Happiness

Marcia K. Morgan

Published by Migima, LLC.
Bend, Oregon.

Migima

Published by Migima, LLC. Bend, Oregon. Printed in the United States of America.

ISBN: 978-0-930413-03-3 (paperback)
ISBN: 978-0-930413-04-0 (ebook)

Library of Congress Control Number: 2020923014

This book contains general information and considerations to help you make a decision about your last name at marriage and is not in any way intended to replace legal advice.

DEDICATION

This book is in memory of Baydon Poochini, our yellow lab.
She laid by my desk, warming my feet and my heart.

TABLE OF CONTENTS

INTRODUCTION

When Kim walked into the Tex-Mex bar that cold night, it changed her life forever. It had been a long week, and the pressure to finish her degree was looming. She savored each take-me-to-a-warm-beach sip of her margarita while reading a book on ancient synagogues in the diaspora. *"Who reads that kind of book in a bar?"* Brendan said as he spotted Kim. Maybe it was fate he was bartending that shift instead of studying history or playing with his band on the local wedding circuit. When he commented on her book, she joked back, *"What does a bartender know about theology?"* These questions were perhaps the oddest pick-up lines in bar lore, but it sparked a conversation between two people who fell in love and got married four years later.

Kim called me a few months before her wedding to Brendan, my nephew. *"I am trying to decide what to do about my last name when we get married,"* she said. *"I'd love your thoughts."* Because I possessed the world's fattest files on married last names, and kept my own name when I married, I was thrilled to explore with Kim what might be a good fit for her.

Since the 1970s, I have cataloged hundreds of magazine articles, notes from blogs and social media, research findings, and letters to the editor discussing married last name quandaries. My files are full of newspaper clippings from complete strangers' weddings (who could forget the Poole-Houzz, Berry-Fields, Day-Knight, Lamb-Ramsey, Easton-West, Black-Brown weddings? Really. You can't make this stuff up). I also have copies of advice columns where young couples are trying to navigate pressing nuptial decisions around wedding reception seating charts, and yes, what to do about their names.

I discovered that this mound of information needed to be organized to help people decide on their married last names. Thus, *Should I Change My Name?* was born.

I continued gathering married name information and stories by conducting dozens of interviews with heterosexual and same-sex engaged and married individuals, and collecting historical data from the library and internet. I found researching and writing this book personally fulfilling, knowing it could help couples solidify their lives together in a way that works for them. I hope the information in this book will also help you and your partner determine what to do with your own names.

The topic of married names may sound a little dry, but believe me, it has all the makings of a made-for-tv movie: romance, history, personal struggles, political fights, international intrigue! What we do with surnames reflects the shifting purpose of marriage in our society, our fluid cultural mores, and rapidly changing gender roles. So, buckle up for an interesting ride.

Should I Change My Name? is for anyone getting married. By the fact you picked up this book, I assume you, too, are trying to decide what to do about your own name. Let's start with a basic principle: there is no right or wrong way to do married last names. There are no laws in the United States that say you have to change or not change your name in any particular way. The name decision is very personal and up to you and your partner.

Part of this book examines the traditional roles of women/brides and last names, which does not necessarily apply to same-sex marriages but may be helpful information nonetheless. Same-sex couples are entering a unique frontier, creating their own "traditions," because they do not have a historical track record of marriage naming practices from which to draw. They also do not share the same socially-prescribed gender roles as in a heterosexual marriage, which strongly influences who gives up a name and who doesn't.

Same-sex couples encounter fewer social expectations regarding married names. Who should take or change whose last name? Should names be changed at all? Now, a couple getting married may consist of two brides or no brides. What about naming children? The name-changing marriage ritual has suddenly been tossed in the air like a bridal bouquet. What do same-sex couples do? What I learned in researching this book may surprise you.

If you don't know what to do about last names, you are not alone. This book contains stories from other people about their experiences with name choices, marriage, and lessons learned. The questions they grappled with may be your questions as well. What are the customs and traditions around married names, why do they exist, and which ones do you want to embrace in your own life? How do both you and your spouse show you have devoted your lives to each other, you are now a family unit, and have come together as equal, loving partners? If you delete your name, how do you avoid losing your identity and sense of self? This isn't the Witness Protection Program where someone's identity disappears but rather a 50-50 partnership, right?

Each name option presented in this book comes with its own suitcase of positive and negative considerations: whether it is using one last name, keeping your own name, creating a new common name for both of you, hyphenating the two last names, using your birth last name as a middle name and adding your partner's name to the end, or having a professional name and a social/private name. Each of these options will be explored in Chapters 4-9. The important thing is that *each* person in the couple feels good about the name choice. It should not be a power struggle nor a decision to go into blindly without understanding the historical-cultural roots and the joys and pitfalls of each option. Names are a big deal.

As a sociologist, I have worked for over 40 years nationally and internationally on gender issues. My interest and curiosity in sex roles and culture piqued as I began examining married naming traditions. I interviewed people who struggled when they changed their name at marriage. Years into the marriage, they changed their names back. Others hyphenated their two last names together but found it cumbersome and later dropped one of the last names. Others kept their birth names at marriage but eased into using their spouse's last names socially and eventually, all the time. Those who researched name options before getting married, who thought about their names, and who discussed their feelings openly and honestly with their partner were happier and much more comfortable with the decision they made right from the start.

You will see that my writing style, a mixture of both head and heart, incorporates research and story-telling. The information is presented in a no-judgment zone—I am not advocating for one naming option over another. I had my own last name journey, which I will share with you throughout the book, and I want you to have yours. My goal is to inform, not to influence your decision. Whatever name you and your spouse-to-be pick, I want you to be happy and excited about joining your two lives together.

In this book, you will learn how to…

- Identify and choose the best name for you and your partner.
- Talk to your partner about name options.
- Find happiness with your name choice.

Legal Advice

I am not a lawyer, but rather someone who studies and researches people's behaviors for a living. This book provides things to consider as you choose your married name. That said, the information should not be taken as legal advice. Rather, if you have questions, unusual or complicated circumstances, please seek the advice of an attorney.

Most examples in the book are based on practices in the United States. However, many engaged couple's questions and concerns about names are universal. The laws in the United States and other countries are always subject to change. Therefore, please check the laws in your area of residence and the location of your wedding, especially if you have a destination wedding.

It is much easier (read: cheaper and less time-consuming) to decide whether or not to change your name *at the time you get married*. However, nothing is permanent. Personal dynamics and preferences change for people and it may be possible to change your name at a later time if you want. A general rule to remember is that you can probably change your surname at any time, as long as you are not doing it for fraudulent reasons.

Terms

Because this book addresses primarily two types of nuptials, heterosexual and same-sex marriage, I will refer to a person's original last name as his or her "birth name," "birth surname," or "birth last name," rather than "maiden name." If the term "maiden name" is used by someone in a quote, I left it that way to reflect their statement more accurately. The term "maiden" literally refers to an unmarried female virgin. Even setting that aside for a moment, every time someone says "maiden name," I picture a fair damsel riding her horse side-saddle to the castle, the scarf at the top of her pointy hat flowing in the wind. Not the image I am going for here.

I also want to be inclusive of all people with my pronouns. I use *they, partner, spouse, prospective spouse,* or *spouse-to-be,* when possible; *he* or *she* when it specifically pertains to male or female. I may also use the pronoun *their* when the subject is singular.

"Née" is a term used to signify a married woman's birth last name. It means "born" in French and is generally put in parenthesis after a woman's current married last name if it is different. For instance, Jane Smith (née Jones) means that Jane took her spouse's last name Smith at marriage, and her birth surname was Jones.

I hope that this book will help facilitate an open discussion for you and your prospective spouse. Don't be surprised if it takes you down a path talking about religion, traditions, culture, gender roles/expectations, and family of origin issues—you know, the hard stuff we often don't talk about but should. These discussions are fundamental and important to undertake before marriage. Have your spouse-to-be read the book as well. Then come together for an honest conversation about names.

Understanding the level of connection that you have, or don't have, with your birth surname is the first step towards deciding what to do when you marry. This insight is illuminating and empowering as you sort through the married name options later in the book.

CHAPTER 1

IDENTITY – THE POWER OF YOUR NAME

"My name is the symbol of my identity which must not be lost"

–Lucy Stone, Suffragist, Abolitionist, 1855

What is Identity?

Your name is the most basic marker of your identity. Identity is your character, existence, and personality wrapped all together into a package with a label, and that label is your name. Your name is what others call you. You turn around, and you respond. It is how people think of you. It is also how you think of yourself. Your name is a powerful expression of who you are. By constant use over many years, its importance increases.

Your name is also how you distinguish yourself from others. In fact, your name was possibly the first baby gift you got when you were born. Aunt Dalia may have made a baby quilt with your name embroidered in the corner. The wall in your nursery may have had your name prominently displayed in block letters. Birth announcements may have been sent to friends and relatives, not only celebrating your arrival but proclaiming your name to the universe. From that day forward, *you become one* with that name.

When people are asked what their name means to them and their identity, men and women often state such things as:

- Individuality—your characteristics that are unique like a fingerprint; qualities that make you different from others
- Continuity—something you've had constantly throughout life
- Character—your persona, soul, spirit, nature, essence
- Definition—something that defines you

Names and identity are permanently intertwined. People only untangle that connection and seek new names when they want a new identity. That is certainly the case for many married couples who desire something to symbolize their new lives joined together. Wanting a new name applies to many other situations as well, such as when someone is getting a gender change/reassignment, a divorce, or running from the law. The reason people want to change their names, and therefore their identity, varies greatly, as we will explore throughout this book.

Why Identity Matters to People

Have you ever had your ID stolen? Using the word "stolen" implies that it is a commodity and something owned by a person. Have you ever had someone call you by the wrong name? How did you feel when your name and identification disappeared or you were dismissed? Most people respond to these questions with words like "unsettled," "violated," "invisible," and "anxious." Identity matters to people.

Everyone sees married name options differently and through their own lens of experience and knowledge. It is not "one-size-fits-all." Some see changing identity as a positive, and others see it as a negative. Some people feel a new name would force them to lose their identity, while others want a new identity to start a fresh phase of their life with their spouse. Both perspectives point out that identity is a powerful force, invisibly residing at the core of our very being.

If someone is young when they marry, they may not be vested in their birth surname and are more open to a new name and identity. Some people want to leave behind connections to a harsh or abusive home life. Others want to sever ties with an estranged family or not carry the name of their absent father. Some brides feel pressure from the groom and his relatives to take his name for *his* family continuity. Many want to start a new identity as a married person and have one family name. They see a name change as the outward expression of that new life and role, leaving behind a past life and status. Changing a name is a tangible way of marking these events.

One woman said she wanted her name to reflect "all of her." Her identity needed to include all the names she has used through the years, like badges she has worn with pride for life's different phases. She used her birth surname along with two husbands' names (one past, one present). She felt if she only used her birth surname, it would not reflect the married years and her role as a wife and mother. She wanted her name to show the family she was born into and the families into which she chose to marry.

Others view married names and identity differently. They equate eliminating one person's name in favor of the other's as a symbol of inequality in a marriage, with one person being subsumed and lost in the identity of the other. They feel the practice of changing names is based on a power imbalance and sexism, and something they don't want to perpetuate. When each person in the couple keeps their birth name, it acknowledges each individual's value and worth. It honors both of their families as well as their own personal and professional lives. They make an outward statement that marriage is the joining of two lives and two identities together while everyone remains whole. As one woman said, "my husband didn't adopt me—he married me."

Wedding ceremonies often acknowledge an identity change through the ritual of lighting a "unity candle." The candle symbolizes the two people becoming one couple. The ceremony begins with two lighted candles, representing the two individuals in the couple. Each person takes the candle representing him or herself, and together, they light the center unity candle with their two individual candles. In some ceremonies, the two individual candles are extinguished after the unity candle is lit, representing that they are no longer single individuals, but a married couple joined together. In other ceremonies, after lighting the unity candle, the two individual candles also stay lit along with the unity candle. This observance represents that they are now a married couple and have *added* marriage to their lives and identities. They do not "blow out" or void their individual identities. These two approaches to the unity candle ritual symbolize important nuances about how identity is viewed in marriage.

You may have a totally different way of deciding what to do with your own identity (and married last name) than your parents, your best friend, or me. That's okay. I think about my own name being with me since birth: My name was there when I embedded gravel in my knee on the playground and stabbed myself with a corsage pin at the prom. It was there when I earned a degree, started a company, traveled the world, bought a house, sobbed uncontrollably at partings, and confronted difficult battles. My husband has had a long relationship with his name, too. When we decided to each keep our birth surnames, it worked for both of us. But my experience may not be your experience. Take some time to explore your own connection with your name and identity.

How Men Feel When Women Share Their Identity

Men rarely change their names when they marry. Yet something else may occur for them. They may now be sharing their own name and identity with a partner. There is little information on how a man feels when his spouse deletes his/her own name and uses his. Do men feel a loss of identity, or is it more of a feeling of pride and connection, an extension of themselves and their identity? Anecdotally, the latter seems to be true. Responses I have heard from men or through wives about their husbands included that some men just assumed their wives would take their names. They felt more like a couple when wives had the same name. Some men felt a sense of being one and a family and a responsibility to protect and provide for her. It isn't easy to know if this was due to sharing a name or simply that they were now married or both. On the other hand, many women I interviewed said that their husbands did not care what they did with their names and that it was up to the women to decide what name they wanted to use.

Avoiding an Identity Crisis

An identity crisis is a time of upheaval where old values and new choices clash or are reexamined. Any shift in identity can be disorienting, leaving you to feel lost and misplaced. Marriage, divorce, death of a loved one, retirement, a new job, a move, and other life changes can spur people to question themselves and ask, who am I? Have I lost/found myself? Has my identity changed? What is my new identity, and is it a good fit from here forward?

The fit of your last name can feel great or like a shoe that pinches. What would you rather wear every day, a fuzzy slipper or a Manolo Blahnik stiletto? Okay, maybe that is a bad analogy, but you get the idea. You want your name and identity to be comfortable and compatible.

Even though marriage is a core identity shift, not every newlywed will experience an identity crisis. Many people are excited and thrilled to take a new name that reflects the shift. A new name can bring with it pride and joy. Others experience a sense of loss or even resentment stemming from a name change. Taking your spouse's last name does not automatically mean the death of your identity and independence, any more than keeping your birth surname means you aren't fully loyal to the marriage. The key to avoiding an identity crisis is to know yourself, to think through the decision about your name, and discuss it with your spouse-to-be.

Internal and external factors can also create a potential identity crisis for newlyweds. A new name or not sharing the same last name with your partner may create a disconnect between who you feel you are and how others now see you. Some people may start referring to you as Mrs. Jeromy Lively. Being identified as Jeromy's wife in this way may feel different because now, you have not only taken his last name but his first name as well. Even though you may be Latisha Horner or Latisha Horner Lively, that name and identity may take a back burner to Mrs. Jeromy Lively. Sometimes women feel invisible and like an appendage to the husband when they meld into a first and last name.

When women see their birth surname as temporary and not really their own to keep for their lifetime, it can impact their self-perception and identity. Women are often taught that at some point, they will be asked to give up their name and replace it with someone else's name. What do these messages, based on gender disparity, say about a woman's value, voice, and role in the marriage? Are women already whole and okay as they are? If so, why do they have to change? What is the psychological impact on your identity when you hear your name is impermanent (contrary to what men learn)?

Some may view it as an honor and sacrifice of love to change their name, while others may view it as an unfair duty.

Changing your birth surname can also feel like you are abandoning the identity you have with your culture and ethnicity. Your name also may be tied to your religion. If you dropped your Jewish surname Levine and now go by your spouse's name of Alvarez, your historical and family connection may feel erased. This shift can create a disconnect with your identity. You may have been born O'Donnell from an Irish Catholic family and now go by Nakaya, your Japanese spouse's last name. Outwardly it can look like you belong to a culture and ethnicity that is not your own. These situations can certainly be a point of pride, but they are also ripe for the incongruity and internal struggle that germinates an identity crisis.

In the BBC News Magazine article, *Why Should Women Change their Names on Getting Married?* author Sophie Coulombeau said that changing surnames had a different impact on her than it did on her husband. She realized that changing her name would make her "first and foremost a wife, while my husband would remain, quite simply, himself."

In this chapter, we explored the personal connection you have with your name as your identity. The next step is understanding the reason and historical context of why people began changing their names at marriage.

CHAPTER 2

HISTORY AND CULTURAL TRADITIONS OF MARRIED NAMES

> *"There is a great deal in a name. It often signifies much and may involve a great principle."*
>
> –Elizabeth Cady Stanton, Suffragist, 1847

If you are like me, you never had a stand-out history teacher. I wish I had. History seemed boring and irrelevant to my young life. However, all that changed as I got older. History started to become relevant and tangible. I began to see the connection between history and how we act today.

In researching this book, I read everything I could find on married last names, yet few things discussed the *historical* reasons why people and brides, in particular, changed their names. Although the articles helped today's couples select a name, it felt like the discussion was being presented in a vacuum.

Historically, women were legally and socially viewed as the man's property, had little power, and few rights. The laws and culture in our country, like many other countries, dictated—make that *mandated*—marriage naming practices over the years. Many oppressive laws have been eliminated over time, yet social practices have been slower to change.

Let's explore the concept of marriage, the origins of last names, and the history of why women were originally made to change their names. Couples who know the history of marriage and surnames may make different decisions about their own names than those who don't. They may want their name choice to perpetuate or reject the history or redefine the naming tradition to be more in line with their thinking and values.

The Changing Role of Marriage

As cold as it may sound, marriage is a contract–a legally binding agreement that recognizes and governs the rights and duties of those involved. There are rules about how to join and how to untangle. I know, not terribly romantic. Marriage is also a social and religious contract with expectations of commitment and loyalty. Marriage was originally between a male and a female. Now in the United States and many countries, it is between two adults of any gender.

There has been a seismic shift in the role of men and women in marriage and the reasons why people get married in the first place. Laws in America have long been influenced by what happens across the pond. In 1663, England's marriage laws were based on the religious doctrine that *"the will of the wife is subject to the will of the husband."* Marriage was viewed as a pragmatic relationship to function in a harsh environment with clearly defined roles and expectations. It used to be about *taking* a wife and living a life of double-standards, submission, deference, sex for procreation, power, and one-sided decision-making. Marriage was for families to create alliances to maintain or increase wealth and power, and propagate the species. Love, as we think of it, may or may not have been part of the picture in the early years.

Most marriages today are based on love and companionship rather than sustenance and economics. By the end of the 1700s, selecting a spouse started replacing arranged, "practical" marriages. Marriage shifted from obedience to an intimate partnership, from an unequal coupling to being a team. It evolved to one of a mutual/equal partnership, with or without children, with two-way emotional intimacy and support expectations. No wonder that today the number one characteristic a bride seeks in a partner is someone who can talk about his feelings. I wish I'd been a researcher in the 1600s and could have asked couples that same question.

Another change around marriage is how weddings have become a big production. Today, the average cost of a wedding in the United States is around $36,000. Couples find themselves stressing over hunting down the perfect dress, the cascading flower arrangements, the wedding cake that defies gravity, and the fairytale wedding locale. Proposals are staged in exotic locations, all caught on camera, with the family hiding in the wings as witnesses. There is even a name for a woman who becomes all-consumed by this grand nuptial undertaking, "Bridezilla." For the record, there is nothing wrong with having the wedding of your dreams. But let's pause for a moment and ask, what does this trend have to do with selecting a last name? Perhaps nothing and perhaps everything. Taking time to discuss and thoughtfully choose a last name can be overlooked in all the wedding hype and activities. Now may be a good time to slow down and decide what is important and meaningful.

Tradition

Several couples I interviewed stated that marriage was about embracing tradition. When it came to women changing their names, they didn't give it a second thought. It was tradition, right? For same-sex couples, the answer didn't come that easily. That got me to think about the concept of tradition and why it is valued in a society. What is tradition? What does it mean? Why are traditions important? How are traditions passed through cultures and generations? Can or should traditions change meaning over time?

Traditions all start someplace. They are concepts and rituals that demonstrate the values of the culture, religion, or ruling party of the time. They are created to provide the contours of a formal, prescribed order through ceremony and social custom protocols. Traditions can help pass along history and communal stability. We also know that Coverture laws in the United States, described in more detail later in Chapter 3, influenced many wedding traditions. Coverture was the legal principle that upon marriage, a woman became her husband's possession.

Traditions can and do change as cultural views and perceptions shift around gender. Some traditions have a long shelf life while others run their course, usefulness, and applicability in today's world. One could argue that it was "tradition" to deny women autonomy, a job, property, their own money, the vote, etc. or that gay men or women could not marry. Gone are the days where couples blindly followed wedding traditions without thinking through what they meant and what they were committing to: "to obey" has been dropped from most wedding vows, asking the father for permission to marry his daughter is not required, and throwing rice at weddings (a sign of fertility, lethal for birds and also a mess to clean up) have all but disappeared at weddings. If you like certain traditions, do them. If you don't, don't do them. But educate yourself about what these traditions mean. Maybe even create one or two new "traditions" that better fit with your values.

It is interesting, and perhaps disturbing, that many Coverture-inspired wedding traditions have remained. For instance, "giving away the bride" is often viewed as a sweet way to honor the bride's relationship with her father. Yet, we know that it originated as part of the property exchange (and name exchange) and was intended to be taken literally. One has to ask why this name-changing tradition is still so prevalent in America and other similar Anglo countries but not in most of the world? Should a "tradition" have inherent caché simply because it has been done for years, or is it time to make a conscious change?

The United States has abandoned many traditions and practices due to a values shift, education, or consciousness such as eliminating burning witches, wearing black face, beating children, etc. Some would argue that the tradition of women giving up their names is clinging to an outdated construct of subservience. If it wasn't, why wouldn't men change their names or both people change their names to establish a "family" name? Taking the husband's last name at marriage has not always been a quaint or romantic tradition. Traditions can be lovely and good or they can embody harm and represent inequality.

Origins of Last Names

Over 6.3 million surnames were recorded in the last United States Census. Yet, historically speaking, surnames are a fairly recent phenomenon and were not considered important for many centuries around the world.

According to legend, the Chinese began using surnames in 2852 BC under Emperor Fu Xi. For the first thousand years, surnames were derived matrilineally but switched to patrilineal during the Shang Dynasty (1600-1046 BC). As will be discussed later, Chinese women today generally do not change their names upon marriage. They use their full birth names or their husbands' surname plus the word for wife. In the past, women's given names were often not used publicly, and women were referred to in official documents by their family name plus the character "Shi." The Chinese list their surname first, followed by their given names.

In Europe, the concept of surnames became popular in the Roman Empire. During the Middle Ages, this practice died out with Germanic, Persian, and other influences. When a man from a lower-status family married a daughter from a higher-status family, he would often adopt the wife's family name.

English surnames appeared more recently. Surnames began being passed down through the patriarchal line about 1,000 years ago and brought by the French around the time of the Norman Invasion in 1066. Before this, the population was small enough that one single name, given to the person at baptism, was enough. However, using one name became confusing as the population grew. Married women did not have their own surname since the Normans brought with them the Doctrine of Coverture. Her state of having no surname reflected this. In the year 1340, a legal court declared, *"when a woman took a husband, she lost every surname except 'wife of.'"*

During the late Middle Ages in Britain, surnames began to emerge in the form of what is called identifier names. These early English-based surnames described one of five things: (1) *Connection to Father*. The "son of John" became Johnson, "son of Peter" became Peterson (common in Northern England), or a simple "s" was added to John, so it became Johns (common in south and west England). MacDonald is Scottish from "son of Donald." (2) *Occupations*. The person's trade, job, or social position became the last name such as Cobbler, Butcher, Smith, Chandler, Taylor, Smith, or Tanner. The last name "Leach" originated from the occupation of physician (since leaches were used to bleed patients). During this time, men began tacking on descriptions to their names such as "Thomas the Cobbler" or "Richard the Baker" to distinguish themselves from others with the same first name. These eventually morphed into surnames. (3) *Geographical Locations.* This often included the place where the person had previously or was presently residing, such as an estate, castle, town, or county (e.g., Kent, Oxford, Cheshire, London, Carlisle). Sometimes the name described the geography of the place (Hill, Marsh, Bush, River). These surnames often had an "At" or "By" before that location, such as Atwater or Bywater. (4) *Public Humiliation.* Some people were given names as punishment for debts and unacceptable behaviors, such as the name Loveless. (5) *Physical or Personal Descriptions of the Person.* This would include such surnames as Short, Little, Black, White, Wise, Young, Gray, Armstrong, or Good. These descriptors often developed into clan or family identifications that became surnames as we know them today.

By 1400, most English used surnames. However, most Scottish and Welsh people did not adopt surnames until the 17th century or later. Henry VIII (reigning 1509–1547) ordered that births be recorded under the father's surname. Around 1538, English church registries began recording surnames.

It is difficult to generalize about Native American surname practices because there are so many tribes and traditions. Native Americans were generally identified by their given name and band/tribe name before European contact. Within a band/tribe, other's kinship relationships were known so the existence of what we now know as a "surname" was unlikely but not impossible. Some Native Americans had one name, while others coupled a name with a descriptor name such as Mankiller, Eagle Heart, Brings-Plenty, etc. Gradually, some of these names were used as surnames by descendants.

Many Native American names changed after the introduction of Christian culture and religion. Yet, there was not one simple process of Native Americans acquiring American/Christian surnames. As governments expanded their oversight of Native nations, having a "White" or "English" name was required for recognition on official documents. It is important to distinguish between a written recording of surnames in official papers (i.e., censuses, tribal rosters, school and church records, treaty signatures, reservation, and Indian agent paperwork, etc.) and the real practices among Native American tribes/societies since they differed markedly. This bureaucracy and the expansion of patriarchal social structures into Indian Country resulted in adopting western family names. After contact with Europeans (and the spread of patriarchy), many Native communities adopted the custom of taking one's husband's surname at marriage.

One Native American woman shared with me that her own name came from a Québécois Catholic man named Hormisdas Archambault. He had settled in the Dakota Territory, married several Dakota women, and produced many children. This Native-European intermarriage resulted in the Archambault surname entering the Native family structure. Although this was not uncommon, it was by no means universal. Today, the Oceti Sakowin (Sioux) have many people with the surname of Archambault.

In early African history, like in many parts of the world, only given names were used and eventually maternal or paternal surnames were added. The continent of Africa is home to hundreds of languages and thousands of different ethnic groups. Some practice tribal religions, others Islam or Christianity. Most people in the north of Africa are Muslim and thus follow Islamic married naming practices. In central and southern Africa, as a result of European colonization, many nations are partially Christian and use European married names practices. This complex background makes summarizing African married naming traditions difficult.

African Americans with relatives who experienced slavery have a complex history with surnames. Surnames played a role in the experience of slavery from oppression to independence. Historians looked at runaway ads, diaries, slave records, bank records, ship manifests, and Freedman's bank deposit records to identify slave surname naming patterns.

When black people arrived in America on slave ships starting around 1619, they were often transported under the shipper's name, or the ship manifest simply described the slave in physical terms (male child, about 12 years old) instead of a first or last name. Generally, enslaved people only used first names or had surnames that went unrecorded or kept secret. If they brought a surname from Africa, it would likely be their mother's or father's surname.

Once in America, it was not unusual for slaves to take the surname of the slave owner or former owner. A surname could also be forced upon them by the slave owner and not be a name of the slave's choosing. This naming process was a way to "brand" them, connecting them to the plantation or place they lived and worked.

Because slaves were considered property and not fully human, they could not legally marry. However, many slave owners did not discourage "marriage" for religious reasons and the belief that married male slaves would be less likely to run away. Additionally, if the woman slave had babies, the children would be the property of the slave owner. Even though slave marriages were illegal, ceremonies and celebrations didn't stop and many slaves adopted the common practice of that time where the wife took the husband's last name. These slave family surnames were generally maintained if the family unit was kept together in proximity. However, many families were separated during slavery (estimated to be about a third of the families), and with that, surnames were lost and changed over time.

After emancipation, many former slaves adopted new surnames. Choosing a surname was part of exercising their newfound freedom. Many did this to have a surname for the first time or to shed the surname given to them by their former master (some kept that name). Many picked a new last name after a person they admired (e.g., Washington, Jefferson) or simply a popular name or person. Some used the surname Freeman or Freedman to distance themselves from slavery and to honor their new status. Even after emancipation, some white people would only refer to African Americans by their first names to disrespect them and their new surnames. You can see how genealogy research of African American married surnames before and after slavery can be challenging.

Changing a surname can be a way to alter identities for political purposes and demonstrate power over marginalized people. As mentioned above, slaves were often forced to erase their African names and take a new name, alienating them from their culture and heritage. Native Americans were forced into assimilation by changing their first and last names with more Anglo-Saxon or Christian roots. Some Jewish people who fled European countries during World War II to escape the Nazis, changed or replaced their surnames under political pressure to avoid persecution.

Married Surname Practices in Other Countries

Changing last names at marriage is not a worldwide, universal practice. Most people around the world do not delete their own surname and change it to their spouse's name when they marry. To say taking a husband's name is "traditional" is technically inaccurate when you look at the rest of the world. Changing a surname at marriage is most common in Australia, Falkland Islands, Gibraltar, India, Ireland, New Zealand, Philippines, the English-speaking provinces of Canada, and the United States. Even in the United States, around 70 - 80% of the newlyweds are "traditional" (taking their spouse's name), and that number is decreasing.

Laws are fluid and constantly changing. Therefore, the information below may be accurate today but maybe not next year. If you are having a destination wedding, moving to another country, or blending cultures with your partner, you will need to confirm the governing laws on marriage and names. Additionally, although a country may have a law stating that all married couples must keep their birth surnames, there are still some "old country" practices and traditions that some families continue to follow.

Let's take a look around the globe at some of the unique naming practices in other countries:

Canada
In most of Canada, either partner may assume the surname of the other upon marriage. However, in the province of **Quebec**, the laws state that women must retain their birth surnames when they marry. They may use their husband's surnames socially, but their legal name must remain the same from birth to death. For a married woman to change her surname to her husband's, she must legally change her name through the courts.

Europe and Scandinavia
Married women commonly keep their birth surnames in **France, Belgium, Italy, Switzerland,** and several other European countries. However, a married woman may use her husband's surname socially/informally.

If you decide to have a destination wedding in a European country (such as Italy), you will want to check on the logistics regarding name changes.

Since 1977 in **Germany**, spouses have been able to retain their own birth surnames, or either spouse may adopt the other's name at marriage. However, they must declare to the government one of the couple's names as the official "family name" (known as Ehename). The family name is generally the surname of the children. A combined name of the couple cannot be used as a family name, but since 2005, it has been possible to have a hyphenated last name as a family name. Up until the late 1970's in German speaking countries (including Switzerland), "Fräu" plus the husband's last name was used for married women. "Fräulein" plus her birth surname was used for unmarried women. If the woman was the wife of a doctor, she was referred to as "Fräu Doktor" plus the husband's last name. This is no longer a common practice.

In 15th-19th century **Holland**, Roman-Dutch Law had a doctrine similar to Coverture. Under it, a wife was legally considered a minor under the guardianship of her husband. Today, people in Holland who get married generally retain their birth surnames. Like many other European countries, they may socially use one family name if they desire but legally their birth surname remains. Additionally, they can register with the "Municipal Basis Administration" to indicate what informal/social name they want to use. If the marriage dissolves, the ex-spouse may continue to socially use the former spouse's surname unless that spouse objects.

Before 2013 in **Austria**, women's last names were automatically changed to their husbands' name at marriage. Now women, or anyone, can keep their surname upon legal application.

Norway has had a significant increase in the number of women keeping their birth surnames when they marry (currently around 20%).

In **Iceland**, a person's last name indicates the first name of his or her father (patronymic) or in some cases mother (matronymic/metronymic). Many common family names in Scandinavian countries indicate the parent-child relationship, such as Hansen (son of Hans) or Johansen (son of Johan), Jakobsson (son of Jakob).

Greece adopted a marriage law in 1983 that guaranteed gender equality between spouses. Women in Greece must keep their birth surnames for their entire life, whether or not they marry.

Since 2014, women in **Turkey** have been allowed to keep their birth surnames at marriage. Before that time, they had to take their husband's name under Turkish Code of Civil Law, which required a married woman to use her husband's surname; or else to use her birth name before her husband's name by applying to the marriage officer or the civil registry office. The Constitutional Court ruled that prohibiting married women from retaining their maiden names violates their rights.

Eastern Europe

In **Slavic** countries, the sex of the person is added to the husband's surname after marriage. For example, "a", "ova" or "nova" is added to the husband's name, or in the case of Hungary, "né" is added.

In **Russia**, most wives drop their surnames and take their husband's surname at marriage. However, either spouse may file legal paperwork to change names or retain birth surnames. Russia is not a common law country, so any name change requires a formal procedure, including an official application to the civil acts registrar.

Since the same registrar also records marriages, it is often done at the marriage ceremony. The couple's marriage certificate has an option of having one common family name or both spouses using their birth surnames. The couple may use either of their surnames or a completely different name. The gender-neutral law also recognizes the couple's right to use the combined family name or retain their birth surname in divorce.

Asia

In **Vietnam, South Korea, Malaysia**, and many other Asian countries, married women keep their birth family surnames throughout their life. Vietnam has about 100 surnames, and three make up 60% of all names in that country. Korea has about 250 surnames, and three of them comprise almost half the Korean population. Additionally, surnames are honored as something inherited from their ancestors.

In **China**, women generally don't change their birth surnames at marriage. There are just a few hundred common Chinese surnames and 20 are shared by half the population. 85% of China's population shared the names Wang, Zhang, and Li. The surname is listed first in the sequence of names and the given name at the end.

India is a large country with many cultures and, therefore, traditions. Indian surnames may often signify caste, village, and occupation and are used along with the given names. The surname may be located in different locations: In northern Indian states, the surname is placed after given names. In parts of southern India, the surname is placed before the given name. It is often shown as an initial (for example, "M" for Madduri). Parts of India have a tradition of putting together several things to make up a name. For instance, a person might use the village name plus the father's first name plus their own name plus caste/occupation name (as first, second, third names, and fourth names, with the village and oc-cupation names optional). In some Indian communities, when a woman marries, she takes her husband's given name as her middle name and also takes his surname. During the marriage ceremo-ny, the husband may change his bride's first name as well. In some areas, colonialism has influenced women to be more westernized and become "Mrs. Husband's Name" after marriage, with her fa-ther's name becoming her middle name.

In **Japan**, family surnames were uncommon except among the aristocracy until the 19th century. The Meiji Restoration in 1868 mandated using surnames. Today there are approximately 100,000 Japanese surnames. A couple may not be viewed as being lawful-ly married if they have different surnames. However, in 2015, the Japanese courts upheld that women could informally/socially use their birth surnames but not legally keep them. Since Japanese writing goes in an up-down vertical manner, the family surname may be referred to as the "upper name."

In **Taiwan**, married women keep their birth surnames. However, it is also legal to take the spouse's surname. Some older women add the husband's surname to theirs as was common in the early to mid-20th century.

In the **Philippines**, married women generally change their names to their husbands' surname, although they are not legally man-dated to do so.

Middle East

The concept of surnames is a relatively modern one. Names were mostly tribal and still are in some regions. The last name might end in "zai" (Pashto) or "zadeh" (Persian) meaning, "from the tribe of, son of, or descendent of." Many women want to retain that connection with their tribe, just as men want to keep their connection.

In 1918, it became mandatory for men and women to use a surname in **Iran**. At that time, the heads of families (mostly men) had the right to choose their family members' (including the wife's) surname. In 1925, Civil Registration Article (4) changed that practice. Now it states that everybody should choose his/her own name. *"The wife... maintains her family name that was called by."* In 1940, another Article (43) was added that said, *"If the couple separate legally, maintaining husband's surname is allowed if the husband allows, and if the husband has taken wife's family name, maintaining wife's surname is allowed if the wife allows."*

In the Arab world, most men and women keep their family names for life, even after they marry. The given or personal name may be a person of inspiration (e.g., Muhammad), then the son/daughter of, then the family name. In **Pakistan, Iran, Bangladesh,** and **Libya**, most women do not change their names when they marry. However, if they wish to change it, they must request a government document to deviate from the custom. If a woman changes her birth surname, it may be viewed as a rejection of her family lineage.

Spanish-Speaking Countries

In Spanish and Portuguese speaking cultures (**Spain, Portugal, Mexico, Venezuela, Chile, Peru,** and other parts of **Central** and **South America**), women do not delete their birth surname when they marry. It is considered impolite towards her family if she changes her name. All men and women have two last names. The first last name is their father's surname and the second last name is their mother's surname. There is generally no hyphen used with the surnames. Children are given both parent's middle or paternal surnames, so the name combination changes with each generation.

If "Juan Gomez Garcia" and "Maria Rios Sanchez" had a child Gabriela, her full name would be "Gabriela Gomez Rios." A 1995 law in Spain allowed parents to choose whether the mother or father's surname goes first. However, all children from the same parents must use the two surnames in the same order.

Compound names in Spanish-speaking countries can sometimes be several words together that must remain together. For instance, José Sanchez Perez y Medina Estrella, has José as his first given name, Sanchez as his middle name, the compound surname Perez y Medina as his first (paternal) surname, and Estrella as his second (maternal) surname. His children, therefore, would inherit the compound surname "Perez y Medina" as their paternal surname. Neither "Perez" or "Medina" alone is a surname and would not be passed on to children.

Years ago, mostly in the upper classes, married women added their husband's surname with the preposition "de" (which means "of") in front of it. That tradition has mostly disappeared. A "de" at the beginning of the last name may also indicate where the family was originally from, such as de Leon, de la Cruz, or de Silva. In **Peru** and the **Dominican Republic**, women normally keep all family names after getting married. For example, if "Angela María Pérez Martínez" marries "Juan Martín De la Cruz Valdez", she will be called "Angela María Pérez Martínez de De la Cruz, and if the husband dies, she will be called Angela María Pérez Martínez Vda. de De la Cruz" (Vda. being the abbreviation for viuda, "widow" in Spanish). In Peru, a law enacted years ago, stated that all married women are allowed to keep their last names if they wish with no alteration.

England, Wales, Scotland, Ireland

In 2014, approximately two-thirds of British women eliminated their birth surnames and took their husbands' last name upon marriage. Recent studies show that number has gotten smaller, although the majority of women still change their names. In Scotland in the 16th century, married women did not change their surnames, but today it is common practice. Additionally, if the woman's family is more prominent or influential than the man's family, he may take the woman's last name.

In English-speaking countries, the usual order of names is "given-middle-surname." However, for cataloging in libraries and citing the names of authors in academic papers, the order is changed to "last, first, middle," with the last and first names separated by a comma, and items are alphabetized by the last name.

World Declarations about Married Surnames

We think of married naming practices as a "local" custom where geographic areas, ethnic groups or countries create their own laws. However, as issues of equality, disparities/discrimination, and gender empowerment began to emerge around the globe, so did issues around married surnames. In 1978, the **Council of Europe** required member governments to adopt equality of rights in transmitting family names. A similar declaration was adopted by the **United Nations**. The problem of gender discrimination around marriage naming practices could not be ignored. Similar measures were adopted by several countries, including West Germany (1976), Sweden (1982), Denmark (1983), and Spain (1999). Legal discrimination cases regarding family names began appearing in the courts. *Burghartz v. Switzerland* challenged the lack of a husband's option to add the wife's surname to his surname when this option was available for women. *Rose v. Switzerland* challenged a prohibition on foreign men married to Swiss women keeping their surname if this option was provided in their national law, an option available to women. *Ünal Tekeli v. Turkey* challenged prohibitions on women using their surname as the family name, an option only available to men. The courts determined these laws violated new international measures.

In 1979, the United Nations adopted the *Convention on the Elimination of All Forms of Discrimination Against Women*, which declared that women and men, and specifically wife and husband, shall have the same rights to choose a "family name."

Same-Sex Marriage

Same-sex marriage has only recently become legal in the United States and several other countries. Consequently, there is little research on what couples are deciding to do about their last names. Through interviews and anecdotal information, I learned that most same-sex couples do not change their names even when children are involved. Same-sex marriages challenge the premise that one person loses and one wins in the "giving up the last name" ritual. Two men or two women have equal caché regarding their last names. The history of ownership (wives as property) is absent from a same-sex couple's discussion of names. They are free from the encumbrance of history, maiden names, and social expectations.

As of this writing, only nine states have an official name change option for men as part of the marriage proceeding, whether in same-sex or heterosexual marriage. The other 41 states have a name petition process through the courts that can be done at any time, like any basic name change, for men who want to change their names. All states have the name change option for women as part of the marriage process. This is one of the last discriminatory laws against men (whether same-sex or heterosexual marriages) who want to change their names. If you are a male who plans to change your name at marriage, please check with the county clerk's office in the county where you are getting married. I predict those laws will be changing soon.

Religion

Some couples turn to religion for guidance on what to do about married last names. Yet, most world religions do not have specific edicts about names. Couples find they must extrapolate information from religious teachings about gender roles within marriage to get a glimpse at what to do.

The following is a brief overview of what some religions say about marriage. It is nearly impossible to generalize about religious beliefs because of the subsets and factions within every religion. Some are more orthodox, taking religious texts literally as fact, while others see texts as historical, using metaphors as lessons to take seriously but not literally. This is not intended to be a comprehensive or scholarly writing on religion but rather to encourage you to start doing your own research, or talk to your faith leader.

In Christianity, marriage is viewed as a sacred and spiritual institution, a covenant. For some, it typifies the relationship between Christ and the church and a bond among husband, wife, and God. The Bible also says that a woman was created from a man. Some would argue that taking his name at marriage symbolizes the belief that they are "one flesh."

The Bible also has many stories and teachings about the hierarchical structure of marriage and the relationship between husband and wife (written in a time when women had few legal rights). The New Testament letter to the Ephesians says that the man is the head of the household and the wife is to be subject to her husband. Husbands are to love their wives as their own bodies and uphold a special responsibility of providing leadership, provision, and protection in their marriage. If the Bible offers guidance on who should be in charge in a marriage, does a name logically follow that directive?

Although the Bible may reference the different roles of men and women in marriage and who was created from whom, the Bible does not directly state that a woman must take her husband's name at marriage. In fact, *there were no last names in the world when the Bible was written.* Women were often identified by where they were born or lived (Mary Magdalene, was from the city of Magdala), by their husband (Sarah, wife of Abraham; Rebekah, wife of Isaac), by their children (Jochebed, mother of Moses), or by their children's occupation (Elizabeth, mother of John the Baptist; Hannah, mother of Samuel the Profit) similar to ways men's last surnames arose from their location, father, or work.

In Islam, most Muslim women retain their family names when they marry and do not change their names. (See Chapter 2, information on countries). This tradition is viewed as a respectful way to honor each family's heritage, history, and linage.

In Jewish tradition, the most important name is the Hebrew name, such as the Son of Emmanuel. When a couple gets married, they sign their Hebrew names on a written contract of "Ketubah." Surnames, as we know them today, are important but considered secondary to Hebrew names. A male's given name is traditionally followed by "ben" (meaning: son of) and the father's name (e.g., Abraham ben Ezekial). A woman's given name is followed by "bath or bat" (meaning: daughter of). "Ben" can also form part of Hebrew names such as Benjamin. Levi ben Yehudah or Adah Bar-Ilan may not literally mean the son and daughter of Yehudah and Ilan, but rather the male and female descendants of men called ben Yehudah and Bar-Ilan.

Today in Orthodox Judaism, most women take their husband's last names upon marriage. In other branches of Judaism, some women take their husbands' last names and some do not. There is nothing in the Torah that states married Jewish women must take their husbands' surnames.

Cultural Messages

Another part of the history around married last names is found in and transferred through pop culture. As young girls, we often embellished our school notebooks by repeatedly writing our fictional future husband's name in the margins, matching our name to his. One week I was the wife of a Beatle (usually Paul McCartney), the next week, I was married to a teenage heartthrob from a television show. With the precision of engraving fine silver, we would carefully print our own first name in front of *his* last name. We would say the new name combination aloud and take it down the aisle for a spin. We might even proclaim our intention to marry this person in about 20 years (unbeknownst to them, of course). How did that name sound? Hum. Marcia McCartney. Not bad. Good alliteration. At that age, we assumed that romance had three simple steps: have a crush, wait to be chosen, and then get married. It seemed logical unless in between, there was an untimely arrest for stalking. Maybe for you, that crush was on Justin Bieber, Michael B. Jordan, Zac Efron, Usher, or any of the Hemsworth or Jonas brothers. I know I was not alone in this odd childhood ritual of practicing deleting my own name and taking my future husband's last name.

This behavior was most on display with my beloved "Roy Rogers and Dale Evans" horse-themed, metal lunch pail that I proudly carried in elementary school. I took white medical tape and, with bold determination, covered over Dale's name. New to using a pen and harnessing ink, I wrote my own name on the tape. Some of it smeared, but it did not diminish the sentiment. Now it read like it should have coming off the manufacturing line, "Roy Rogers and Marcia Morgan." I still have that lunch pail, and the tape is still hanging on. (As an aside, Dale did not take Roy's last name when they married. It was also her fourth marriage.)

Surveys show that some American women who take their husband's last names do it for what is described as "romantic reasons." How does a behavior get labelled as being romantic? How is a romantic gesture created and marketed? Rubbing noses may be popular in parts of Alaska but not Atlanta. Giving your love a spoon in Wales is serious stuff but is met with odd looks in Wisconsin. Presenting a Diary Day Planner is heart pounding in South Korea but oddly received in San Diego. How we define romance is heavily influenced by the culture via the media and popular images (advertising, television, movies, and songs). For example, diamonds were not typically used in wedding rings (colored stones were the norm) until Debeers had an advertising campaign in 1947, convincing Americans that only "diamonds are forever" and meant true love.

After World War II, magazine ads showed women contently being housewives. They wore high heels and pearls, vacuumed with glee, made the perfect meal in the perfect house with 2.5 kids. Rosie the Riveter was put on the back burner. Cultural images are powerful and persuasive: Your prince will come. Marriage is the prize. Life will be good.

Cultural norms and values are also canonized through music. The following is a sampling of songs that romanticize the idea of a woman giving up her name and replacing it with her husband's name. At times, the marriage name swap is viewed as an accomplishment. It is elevated to the level of winning, succeeding, or increasing one's status. Some songs talk about the power and commodity of the name when a woman takes her name *back* after a divorce. The song title is listed along with the name of the performer or lyricist.

- "Change your Name" Chase Bryant
- "My Last Name" Dierks Bentley
- "Last Name" Carrie Underwood
- "Got My Name Changed Back" Pistol Annies
- "Marriage" Marques Houston
- "Island Song" Larry W. Jones
- "Love Like This" Jay Sean
- "Whoa" Jaheim
- "Alone" Bahamas
- "Hey You" Shakira
- "Sensitive New Age Guys" Christine Levin
- "I Believe in You" Snoop Dog
- "My Name is My Name" Pusha T
- "First Name Initial" Annette Funicello
- "Viola" Nikola Sarcevic
- "Kerosene" Miranda Lambert
- "Foolish" Meaghan Trainor
- "It's a Love Thing" Keith Urban
- "Please" Toni Braxton
- "Language of Flowers" Tara Mascara
- "Where Blacktop Ends" Rhett Akins
- "Ugly Face" Glenn Lewis
- "Teenage Love Affair" Alicia Keys
- "Sign Your Name" Terence Trent D'Arby (lyrics)
- "The Wedding Song" Noel Paul Stookey
- "Come Close" Mary J. Blige, common
- "Slow Down" Bobby Valentino
- "These are Things" Wheat
- "Bus Stop" The Hollies
- "I Don't Want to Be a Bride" Vanessa Carlton

CHAPTER 3

COVERTURE

What is Coverture?

Coverture is a word you probably don't know. If you are trying to decide what to do about your last name, *you should know all about it*. If you only get one thing out of this book, I hope it is understanding Coverture—what it was, why it was implemented, and how it impacted (and continues to impact) married last names. The laws of Coverture required women to take their husband's last names. If they didn't, there were legal, social, and quality of life consequences. Coverture *to this day* is at the core of the tradition why women in the United States change their names when they marry.

Coverture was a set of laws in the United Kingdom and the United States for many years. It was derived from feudal Norman custom (Norse Viking settlers in France) who brought the common law concepts to England around the Middle Ages. Coverture was a legal doctrine whereby, upon marriage, a woman's legal rights and obligations were *subsumed* by her husband, and she literally belonged to him. When she was born, she was under her father's identity, and when she married, it was transferred to her husband. It held that no female person legally existed. She was a legal non-entity and was denied a separate legal existence from her husband. A woman was often proud to bear his name because it gave her some status in a society of male-run courts, churches, and governing bodies. Through marriage, the husband and wife became one flesh and blood, *one person* in law (and that person was the husband).

Coverture literally means "covered by." A married woman's legal status was called "*femme couverte*" (covered women). An unmarried woman was called "*femme sole*" (absent of husband). After marriage, all of a woman's rights as a person disappeared under the pretense that "property cannot own property," and she was property. Not only was a married woman not allowed to own property, but she also could not vote, she could not file lawsuits or be sued, enter into contracts, keep her own wages, serve on a jury, control or acquire wealth, exercise ownership over real estate, participate in business, maintain any rights over her children, and other restrictions. She also could not keep her surname. If she left or divorced her husband, there was a good chance she would never see her children again since he owned them. Any property she owned before marriage was handed over to the husband. He could use, sell, or dispose of her property without her permission. She also had no legal rights over her body, which meant her labor, "products" of her body (children), or sexual access. Her husband could also rape her. Legally he could not kill her, but he could beat her ("rule of thumb" meant he could hit her with anything that was not bigger than his thumb – as an aside, that is why I never use this expression).

Now we get to the issue of last names. Since the Doctrine of Coverture stated a woman lacked an independent legal identity apart from their husband, she received her father's last name when she was born until she was literally "given away" at marriage. Once married, the woman took her husband's last name in the property transfer. She was now labeled as *his* property.

Around **1605**, historian William Camden identified women who wished to keep their surnames as filling the marriage with "ambition, pertness, and forwardness." All of these characteristics were socially undesirable traits for a woman at the time.

In March **1776**, Abigail Adams saw an opportunity to talk about Coverture and women's rights in a famous letter to her husband, President John Adams. At the time, he and the Continental Congress were deciding what the new America would look like. *"In the new Code of Laws which I suppose it will be necessary for you to make, I desire you would remember the ladies, and be more generous and favorable to them than your ancestors. Do not put such unlimited power into the hands of the husbands. Remember all men would be tyrants if they could."*

Abigail was friends with another Continental Congress member's wife, whom she called a "Sister Delegate." They decided to tell their husbands of this newly created title and, at the same time, put in a dig regarding married last names. *"Why should we not assume your titles when we give you up our names?"*

Coverture played a major role in influencing the women's right to vote movement in the United States. Some argued that only women who owned property should have the right to vote, and Coverture excluded married women from owning property (relatively few women were unmarried or widowed). In other words, few adult women would be eligible to vote. It was a "Catch 22." Some people felt the right to vote should be available for all women since all [white] men could now vote whether or not they owned property.

Slowly, the Coverture laws in the United States began being chipped away. In **1871**, the Supreme Court took up whether Coverture's main purpose was the legal subordination of women, specifically through marriage, and whether it violated the Constitution's 14th Amendment (equal protection under the law). Women's nonexistent legal status on many matters, including keeping their birth surnames, was a predominant issue.

Before President Theodore Roosevelt married his first wife in **1880** (she later died in childbirth), he stated, *"As regards the laws relating to marriage, there should be the most absolute equality preserved between the two sexes. I do not think the woman should assume the man's name."* In **1933**, Frances Perkins became the first woman appointed to the United States Cabinet as Secretary of Labor under President Franklin Roosevelt. She was married and chose to keep her birth surname. Many women cheered, while conservatives resented her actions and public visibility.

In **1966**, the U.S. Supreme Court in the *United States v. Yazell* said, *"the institution of Coverture is ... obsolete."* In a separate opinion in the same case, Justice Hugo Black and two of the nine justices said, *"though the husband and wife are one, the one is the husband."* They questioned why a married woman is without the ability to make her own contracts and conduct her own business. Black described modern Coverture as an *"archaic remnant of a primitive caste system."* Male privilege within marriage began to dissipate as Coverture was challenged.

Another interesting law affecting last names was based on the concept of "Bastard Inheritance." This originated from English law and was present in the United States until the **1969** Family Reform Act, which allowed a bastard, a child born out of wedlock, to get an inheritance from parents through wills and other legal documents. Initially, to prove a male child had a direct lineage to the father and be the rightful heir to inheritance, the child had to have the *same last name* as the father. Without the father's name, the child was considered illegitimate. The only way for the child to get the father's name was for the mother to be married to the father (spoiler alert: a name still doesn't prove he was the father). Although some countries still only allow family property to be passed to the male offspring (that could be a whole other book), the concept of using the father's name for a male child is now a moot point since lineage can be proved for a male or female child through DNA.

In the **1970s,** women often kept their birth surnames at marriage as an outward rejection of Coverture and repression and as a show of equality. It is understandable. Women were living and breathing Coverture's oppression in their lives. The primary goal of the women's rights movement in the United States was to establish basic property rights for women even if they were married, which went to the core of Coverture. Many believed that these legal reforms, and others such as forced name changes, as important to achieving equity between the sexes. During this "second wave of feminism," women continued fighting against states that still had laws not allowing women to keep their birth surnames. Many of these women trailblazers helped pass laws around access to voting, bank loans/credit, getting passports, and other roadblocks based on retaining their own names.

During Coverture, a married woman also did not have individual legal liability for criminal actions since it was assumed she was acting under her husband's *orders*. She had no independent thought or will. It was felt that women needed to be protected and provided for. As recently as **1972,** two states allowed a wife accused of a crime to offer a legal defense that she was obeying her husband's orders. Additionally, a husband and wife were not allowed to testify either for or against each other since property cannot testify against its owner. When a woman's husband died, all his property went to the closest male relative and not to her. Even the property she brought to the marriage was no longer hers. Many women became destitute in widowhood. Coverture remained a powerful tool of marital inequality—from married names to legal status—for decades. Women weren't even allowed to sit on juries in all 50 states until **1973.**

In **1975**, the United States Supreme Court struck down a Tennessee law in *Dunn v. Palermo* that required a woman to change her name to their husband's name before she could register to vote.

In **1979,** Louisiana became the last state in the United States to have its "Head and Master" marriage law struck down. The United States Supreme Court in the **1980** *Kirchberg v. Feenstra* decision stated the practice of "male-rule in marriage" was unconstitutional, instead favoring a co-equal structure.

If you think Coverture is ancient history, think again. After the rise of the women's rights movement in the **mid-19th century**, Coverture came under increasing criticism as oppressive towards women. It prevented them from exercising ordinary property rights and entering many professions. Coverture was modified by the **late-19th century** by the passage of the Married Women's Property Act. However, certain aspects of Coverture (mainly preventing a wife from incurring financial obligations so her husband wouldn't be liable) survived as late as the **1970s** in parts of the United States. This included such things as women being unable to get a loan without her husband's consent. I personally experienced that in the mid-**1980s** when my business partner, also a woman, and I went to get a small loan on a building we wanted to buy. Every bank in the city rejected our request because we refused to have a man sign with us. We finally found a credit union that gave us the loan.

In **1982,** Alabama was the last state that wouldn't allow women to retain their birth surnames at marriage. In **1983,** women in Maryland were no longer prevented from voting unless they took their husbands' names. It wasn't until **1993** that all 50 states made it illegal for a man to rape his wife. The remnants of Coverture exist today in more subtle ways in real estate, utility accounts/billings, or banking transactions (men's name first, listed as the "primary," etc.)

Until the early **2000s,** it was common practice in American banks and financial institutions to ask patrons their mother's maiden name as a security question, thus allowing them access to their accounts. The practice in itself is an interesting commentary on how women's birth surnames are well-hidden and not known outside the family once someone gets married. Women's former names were obscure and difficult to find. Today that question is rarely used since genealogical information is easily found online.

The configuration of American families is evolving and not solely defined by last names or a male as the primary figurehead. The United States Census used to ask citizens to identify the "head of the household" in their home, a subjective question, to say the least. What did they mean by head? A man? The person whose name the rest of the family used? The person making the most money? The person tending the children? Cooking the meals? Making the household decisions? Managing the budget? The oldest male with the same last name as the children? The head of household question was dropped from the census in **2001** due to public pressure saying it was antiquated, gender-biased, and irrelevant. It also had an undercurrent of Coverture and the "Head and Master" marriage laws. As an aside, women today are the sole "breadwinners" in approximately 41% of American households and over 38% of women earn more than their husbands in two-parent households.

I would be remiss at this point if I didn't mention the late United States Supreme Court Justice Ruth Bader Ginsburg ("RBG"). She died in **2020**, during the time I was writing this book. A tiny woman, 5' 1" tall and 110 pounds (who did daily push-ups and planks at age 87), made such an impact in our everyday lives. If you are a woman and paid for this book with a credit card in your own name, thank RBG. Without her lifelong work fighting for women's rights, men and women today would not have equal protections. In her own life and career, she battled sexism, founded the Women's Rights Project at the ACLU where she became general counsel, and sat for 27 years on the Supreme Court. The Women's Rights Project took on hundreds of cases seeking to persuade the courts that the 14th Amendment that guaranteed equal protection applied not just to racial and ethnic minorities but to women as well. She led the fight in the courts to address state and federal laws that restricted what women could do, barring them from jobs, and even jury service. Thanks to Ruth Bader Ginsburg, Americans are no longer denied opportunities and basic rights based on their gender. People of all ages, especially women, poured out into the streets when her passing was announced. A make-shift memorial and vigil grew in front of the Supreme Court building in Washington, D.C. Thousands of men and women paid their respects throughout the night and into the coming days. It was powerful and moving. It was also a great loss.

Knowing the history about married last names and Coverture now gives you a context about naming traditions. Educating yourself and others about these roots may influence what you do about your own name when you get married.

Lucy Stone (1818 – 1893)
Let me backtrack a moment to tell you about an important women's advocate who lived during Coverture. Her efforts are so pivotal to the discussion of married last names that she deserved her

own separate section. Suffragist and abolitionist Lucy Stone lead the first efforts to allow women to keep their own names after marriage. Stone was the first known woman in the United States to legally keep her own last name in 1855.

Lucy Stone criticized marriage *"because it gives the custody of the wife's person to her husband, so that he has a right to her even against herself."* Stone kept her last name as a protest against all manifestations of Coverture. She stated, *"a woman should no more take her husband's name than he should hers."* This was the first public challenge of taking a husband's surname at marriage.

Stone was married to Henry Blackwell (whose sister was Elizabeth Blackwell, the first woman in the United States to graduate from medical school). Stone was the first woman in Massachusetts to earn a college degree. Lucy and Henry were a highly visible and controversial couple in their time. They declared that the practice of a woman being forced to change her name *"refused to recognize the wife as an independent, rational being."*

In **1851**, many anti-slavery activists didn't want the institution of marriage to look like one of slave-master. Lucy and Henry stated that the relationship between wife and husband should be one of equality. In their vows, they stated that they intended to *"disobey all laws that refuse to recognize the wife as an independent rational being and confer upon the husband as injurious and unnatural superiority."* They dropped the word *obey* from their wedding vows, and Blackwell declared he stood for equality in marriage. Stone would sign her name *"Lucy Stone (only)"* and if questioned, *"Lucy Stone, Wife of Henry Blackwell."*

Feminist and suffragist Elizabeth Cady Stanton took her husband's surname and signed her name Elizabeth Cady Stanton or E. Cady

Stanton (not Mrs. Henry B. Stanton as was customary). In **1847**, she wrote that *"the custom of calling women Mrs. John This and Mrs. Tom That and colored men Sambo and Zip Coon, is founded on the principle that white men are lords of all."* In 1860, in addressing the judiciary committee of the New York state legislature in "A Slave's Appeal" speech, she stated, *"The negro [slave] has no name. He is Cuffy Douglas or Cuffy Brooks, just whose Cuffy he may chance to be. The woman has no name. She is Mrs. Richard Roe or Mrs. John Doe, just whose Mrs. she may chance to be."* (A "cuffy" was a reference in that era to a negro person/slave).

In **1879**, Lucy Stone was not allowed to vote in the Boston school elections because she refused to use her husband's name on her signature. She was also unable to buy land without signing her husband's name. She continued her very public pressure to allow women to keep their names. Women's rights activist Elizabeth Cady Stanton wrote, *"Nothing has been done in the women's rights movement for some time that has so rejoiced my heart as the announcement by you of a woman's right to her name. It does seem to me a proper self-respect demands that every woman may have some name by which she may be know from cradle to grave."* Suffragist Susan B. Anthony said of Stone, *"I am more and more rejoiced that you have declared, by actual doing, that a woman has a name and may retain it throughout her life."* Lucy Stone died in **1893,** 27 years before American women won the right to vote.

In **1921**, Stone's public fight for a woman's right to keep her name inspired Ruth Hale to found the Lucy Stone League. Hale was a journalist who covered World War I from Paris for the Chicago Tribune. The League, open to both men and women, included many prominent women in society. They worked to make it legal for a woman to keep her birth surname if she so chose. Lucy Stone had a strong and vocal following. Many women who joined the cause of social justice and women's rights came to be known as "Lucy Stoners." The term had negative connotations and was viewed as a derogatory reference except by those who supported the movement.

The "Lucy Stoners" challenged laws and practices in federal courts that refused to recognize a married woman by the name she chose to use other than her husband's. Their slogan became *"My name is my identity and must not be lost."* During the **1920s**, the Lucy Stoners successfully got passports, voter registrations, bank accounts, and real estate deeds issued in the names that the women had chosen. It was a long battle for the women and suffragists (often one and the same) who were publicly bullied, jailed, harassed, and injured. The Lucy Stoners were called names such as *"oddball," "sick,"* and *"in need of a psychiatrist."* However, by **1972,** many legal cases had concluded and confirmed that women could use their birth surnames in whatever ways they wished. The Lucy Stone League made significant accomplishments and took a rest.

Many other women challenged social norms over the years regarding their own identity and married last names. Even Amelia Earhart was called "a staunch Lucy Stoner" by Time Magazine in **1931**. The New York Times referred to Earhart as "Mrs. George Putnam" when covering her historical flights, as was the customary practice in society and publications. In **1932,** Earhart sent a letter to the New York Times requesting she be called by her professional name, Amelia Earhart. Many amazing and accomplished women in their own right were referred to by their husband's first and last names with a "Mrs." put on the front. This "Mrs. Husband's Name" developed in the 19th century as a status reference for wealthy women and gradually adopted throughout the social strata. Yet, many viewed the "Mrs. Husband's Name" as a holdover from Coverture.

In **1950**, Jane Grant and 22 others revitalized the Lucy Stone League. Grant founded The New Yorker Magazine and was the city room's first woman reporter at the New York Times newspaper. The League took on several issues, including the United States Census Bureau that said a married woman could not use her birth surname as her official name in the Census. They were successful in getting that changed. In the **1950s** and **1960s,** the League expanded its scope to focus on all discrimination against women and was the forerunner to the National Organization for Women (N.O.W.). Grant died in **1972,** bequeathing 3.5 million dollars to the University of Oregon, Center for the Study of Women in Society. The minutes from the early Lucy Stone League and other historical documents are housed there.

When I was a doctoral student at the University of Oregon, I spent hours in the archives reading letters and meeting notes from the Lucy Stone League. Many of the 5,000+ League members at the time were wealthy east coast socialites. Their writings demonstrated an intense yet politically-savvy passion for their cause. With white gloves on, I carefully sifted through the documents, getting transported into another time not that long ago. I couldn't help but smile as I read about their "teas." The women planned their super-hero strategies to fight gender discrimination while sipping tea in lovely flowered china cups—how unassuming and civil. The bone china may have been fragile, but not these women. I often think of them as I have my morning tea. I hope you will too. They took the blows and paved the way for all of us to have options. Without them, we wouldn't have a choice to pick the married last name we want to use.

CHAPTER 4

NAME OPTION #1: KEEP YOUR LAST NAME

The Six Most Popular Married Last Name Choices

Is marriage a name-changer? Well, yes and no. Whether you and your spouse change your names is totally up to the two of you. Even though there is no longer a law that says a woman must change her name to her husband's, having so many options for both partners can feel overwhelming and confusing. The decision to change or not change your name carries significant weight and is influenced by many things such as social norms, where you live, what your friends and colleagues do, religion, family, and traditions. Let's help narrow things down a bit.

It is hard to talk about name options without addressing the elephant in the room: most people believe last names are a burden solely for women to think about and do the changing. One woman asked, *why do we have to hold everything together and do all the merging? What about "co-solidarity" between spouses? If I change my name, it is just me showing that solidarity. What about him?* (Surveys show that most men have no interest in changing their own last names and are rarely even asked to consider it. Consequently, most men simply have not thought much about married names.) It was clear from my interviews and the articles I read, typically appearing in women's magazines I might add, that women put much more time and energy into thinking about married last names and feel the responsibility of that decision more than men.

As long as women experience and accept this message, the professional, personal, and emotional costs are disproportionally carried by them. There is nothing subtle about the values in that message.

Journalist Jill Filipovic has written about how girls are taught that their names are temporary and not really their own. This message can impact their perception of their role in society and their understanding of their own value. One woman shared that she remembered learning she would have to change who she is when she got married, but her brothers did not. That message made her feel like she was not okay, but they were. She said she asked herself, why do I need to become someone else, but the boys don't have to? Another woman asked, why should I wipe my life clean like I never existed?

A study of unmarried college students found that most women planned to keep their surnames in some fashion (retain, hyphenate, "maiden to middle") after marriage. Most college men said they did not want their future wives to keep their names. Since most women take their husbands' names, there is some kind of power shift occurring between preference and final decision. What is happening in the discussions couples are having about names? Are women not being heard or their opinions/values not being honored? Are women more easily persuaded? Are women more likely to avoid confrontation and take the peace-keeping role with their future spouse? Do women feel less connected to their birth names than men do? Do women change their minds as it gets closer to their wedding day?

Brian Powell, Professor of Family and Gender at Indiana University-Bloomington, has studied marriage naming practices. He found that whenever a last name is changed, there exists an element of inequality. That is, if a couple sits down to talk about their married last name options, almost always someone has to give. There is an element of power that shifts, and that shift is most commonly influenced by gender.

In the next several chapters, we will discuss the six most common married last name options including, separate, merged, linked, and newly created names. They are:

1. Keep Your Last Name
2. Take Your Spouse's Last Name
3. Use Your Birth Surname as Your Middle Name and Add Your Partner's Surname as Your Last Name
4. Hyphenate Last Names
5. Create New Last Name
6. Use a Professional Name and a Social Name

Choosing a name is both a rational and an emotional decision. Therefore, we will examine each option in depth so you can determine which one feels like the best match for you and your partner. It is rare to find a name option that meets 100% of your lifestyle criteria, but by taking the time to think through each one, you are more likely to make an informed and ultimately better decision.

A "Description" of the six name options, along with the "Benefits and Challenges," is listed below each option. This information was gleaned from multiple sources, including magazine and newspaper articles, online blogs, public comment sections in social media, advice columns, and research studies. Additionally, I conducted dozens of interviews with individuals and couples in various states of matrimony: before getting married, after getting married, those divorced or widowed, and those who had multiple marriages involving multiple last names. I met with people who were straight, gay, and from different races, religions, and cultures. They all shared their experiences, both good and bad.

You will also find a "Review" section for each option that includes women and men's comments from these same sources. The purpose of these reviews is to hear couples' real-world experiences and what they learned from their name choices. You may even hear your own voice in their words. Although this is not empirical research, it will hopefully give you the gist of what some couples have felt and experienced.

Think of reading these reviews like "Trip Advisor" (only it is "Name Advisor") for couples getting married. There are no star ratings, but the comments are honest and raw — some may resonate with you, and some may not. Many people eagerly changed their names and loved sharing their spouse's name while others were anguished and grieved over the identity change. The names, identifiers, and locations of the people in these reviews have been changed to protect their privacy. For the sake of brevity, some comments have been paraphrased and shortened. Since not as many people selected name options 4, 5, and 6, there are fewer review comments listed. Additionally, there are examples of what a person's name would look like, before and after marriage, using that particular option.

Description of Name Option #1

In Name Option #1, each person in the couple keeps their own last name when they marry. No names change. It is estimated between 10% - 25% of women in the United States keep their birth surnames at marriage. Those who choose this name option express interest in gender equality, a value system of fairness, and a desire to pass along both family names. Additionally, their reasons revolve around professional/career, identity, and a desire for simplicity and practicality. Americans are also getting married older, having fewer children, earning degrees, and building a personal and professional life. Consequently, it is more challenging to "let go" or walk away from a name, identity, and reputation.

The number of women keeping their surnames had an upswing in the 1970s, plateaued, and is now making a comeback in popularity bolstered by the preferences of young people. Many people today state they do not see a reason or advantage to changing a lifelong name. Changing names can be a hassle, unnecessary, expensive, inconvenient, and time-consuming. Some social scientists theorize that this may be due to more couples living together before marriage and being comfortable as a unit with two different last names. Option #1 is a popular name option for millennials and same-sex couples.

Who are the people who keep their names at marriage? To answer that question, researchers have looked at gender, age, the difference in age between partners, race, education level, occupation, incomes of husband and wife, etc. The biggest predictor of a woman keeping her birth surname is her education level. Some theorize that the more education, the more egalitarian views about gender and marriage. Of the women who keep their birth surnames, approximately 12% have master's degrees, 21% have professional degrees and 33% have doctoral degrees. Women who have bachelor's degrees are 1.7 times more likely to use a name other than the husband's than those without bachelor's degrees. Those with master's degrees are 2.8 times more likely and doctoral degrees 9.8 times more likely than those with education levels less than a bachelor's degree. This trend is only likely to continue. In 2018, more women than men earned college degrees

(141 for women to every 100 men). By 2027, 151 women to every 100 men will earn college degrees. Women working in academia are also more likely to keep their names.

Age can also be a factor. The median age for women getting married in the United States is 27.8 years old and 29.8 for men. A Harvard University 2005 study found that for each year a woman puts off marriage or having a child, the chances that she would change her name declined about 1%. The age factor was confirmed in a 2009 study by *The Knot* that found women who kept their birth surnames tended to marry older. For instance, if she got married between ages 35-39, she was 6.4 times more likely to keep her name than those married between ages 20-24. They also found that many women who kept their names had or were building a career/profession.

University of Florida researcher and professor Diana Boxer found that married naming practices often reflect attitudes about ex-pected gender roles, especially for women. She also looked at re-gret around name choices. What emerged was that women who retained their birth surnames at marriage were overall satisfied with that choice. Women who changed their surnames were also comfortable with their decision yet were more likely to regret that decision. Some of the reasons are listed in the review section below. A survey conducted by The Telegraph, Business Insider, found that 31% of young wives disliked their married names and wished they had kept the last name with which they were born.

Movie stars and celebrities have long retained their birth surnames, or their created stage names, upon marriage(s). Their name is their identity, product, and brand, as well as their trademark and income producer. Changing their name would be like starting over. Celebrities such as Chrissy Teigen, Heidi Klum, Sarah Jessica Parker, Halle Berry, Mary J. Blige, Jessica Alba, and many others have kept their surnames upon marriage. Vice President Kamala Harris and her husband Douglas Emhoff have different last names (a first for a President or Vice President). Anthropologist Margaret Mead got lots of press in the 1920s when she married her husband, Luther Chessman, and kept her last name. The bottom line is that many people, professional or not, want to keep their "name brand." They want their name consistent and easy to remember, pronounce, and repeat. Demetria Guynes is now Demi Moore. Peter Gene Hernandez is now Bruno Mars. Belcalis Almanza is now Cardi B. Stefani Joanne Angelina Germanotta is now Lady Gaga. Cherilyn Sarkisian is now Cher. Need I say more?

Benefits of Name Option #1

1. Easier Not to Change Your Name

- **Less hassle, time, and expense.** You basically don't have to do a thing. There are no "change" forms to fill out such as legal records, doctor records, driver's license (no standing in line at DMV!), credit cards, bank accounts, business cards, vendor accounts, clients, utilities, insurance, brokerages, mortgage payments, employer, passports, social media handles, voter registration, credit/debit cards, autopay accounts, magazine subscriptions, online forms, memberships, frequent flyer points, club cards, prescriptions, subscriptions, work or school documents to change. If your email address(s) has your last name in it, there is no need to make changes. There is also a monetary savings when you keep your birth surname since some places charge to make changes. Although you may want to get a few certified copies of your marriage license to add your spouse onto certain documents, you will need fewer copies if you don't change your name.

One woman shared that she heard some brides don't change their names to be more "practical." But what could be more practical than not changing anything? Not changing anything is less confusing.

- **Less problem with records.** Government records such as social security, are less likely to get messed up if you use the same name throughout your life, from the cradle to grave. Sometimes you may not discover there is even a problem with your records until 30-40 years later requiring you to painstakingly reconstruct your work or other history.

- **No passport problems on honeymoon.** If you go on your honeymoon outside the United States, you may have problems with your passport and airline ticket if you changed your name and the names don't match your passport or tickets. There is typically not much time to change things between the wedding and honeymoon. These problems are avoided when everyone keeps their birth surname.

2. **Wish to Retain Identity**

- **Continuity.** There is continuity and comfort in maintaining a lifelong identity. When everyone keeps their names, it reduces the chances of an identity crisis.

- **Maintains culture and heritage.** A name can be a badge of one's cultural identity and a link to ancestors. A person's original surname reflects and honors his/her culture and ethnicity. One woman shared that her name is her heritage and keeps her connected to her family roots. She regarded changing her name to her husband's as being absorbed into his family and losing that connection. She is Asian, and he is Italian. As a result, she was never comfortable being addressed as Mrs. His-Italian-Name.

- **Maintain family/social status.** People who had families/relatives who were famous or prominent are more likely to keep their birth names to retain that connection.

3. Consistent with a Person's Personal Values

- **Keeping your birth surname is consistent with your egalitarian philosophy and values.** It symbolizes equality in the marriage. It makes a statement rejecting inequality, sexism, marital hierarchy, and the old laws of Coverture based on ownership and repression of women. It subverts traditional gender role stereotypes. If I take my husband's name, accepting the "custom" without blinking an eye or questioning it, some women ask am I perpetuating an oppressive practice upon which this naming tradition originated? Marital name change patterns are a window into attitudes towards gender, power, and equality. As one woman said, *"I feel keeping my name gives an equal representation in the family."*

It reflects your value system that many marriage traditions, including changing last names, are no longer relevant since they are based on heteronormative "rules" and attitudes. The assumption that all marriages are between a man and a woman has changed in much of the world. Is changing a last name in marriage even necessary in the eyes of others whether in same-sex or heterosexual marriages? When two men or two women keep their own names in a same-sex marriage, it may be a symbolic gesture of resisting heteronormativity.

- **Marriage should be value-added, rather than an act of losing something.** Getting married is a happy, positive experience. Yet to some, losing a name can feel like a loss of selfhood. As one woman said, choosing a partnership shouldn't mean you are giving something up. Where is the *partnership* in that?

When I got married, I kept the first and last name I was given at birth. Being Marcia Morgan all my life, even as I entered a new phase of being married, felt normal and natural. It was also much easier since I didn't have to fill out a single change of name form. Keeping my name helped me in my work since I was already published, appeared in the media, and had started my career as Marcia Morgan. It kept me in touch with clients and long-lost friends since my name had not changed. To me, eliminating my name did not diminish my commitment to the marriage or the love I have for my husband. He was the value-added to my life, not his name.

- **Symbolizes strength and independence.** Research shows a person who keeps his/her birth surname is viewed by others as strong, capable, and self-assured. It establishes credibility on your own and not reliance on your spouse's name, social status, position, etc.

- **Keeps marital status private.** No one knows if you are married or not. This could be a benefit (or a challenge), but why does anyone need to know?

4. Prefer Own Last Name to Spouse's Name

- **Pronunciation and meaning.** Sometimes the people getting married may like their own last name better than their spouse's name and don't want to give it up. Their spouse's name may be

hard to pronounce, have bad associations, or a double meaning (sexual, derogatory, etc.). One woman shared that her husband's last name is "Orr," and people are constantly asking him,
"Or what?" That was a small, albeit humorous, piece of the picture in her decision to keep her birth surname. Not taking the
name avoids these moments.

- **How it sounds with the first name.** The potential new married surname may not sound good with the person's first/given
name. For instance, the bride's first name may be the groom's
last name. Lauren Bush Lauren? In other words, the person's
first name sounds better with their original birth surname.

- **Problems with a spouse's family.** The person getting married
loves their future spouse but not necessarily his/her family.
Consequently, they don't want to be affiliated with that family
through the name.

5. **Professional Advantages**

- **Continuity.** Keeping your surname can help ensure professional continuity. A consistent name while your career is in
full swing is better since you won't lose the value gained from
networking, reputation, speeches, publications, jobs, and experience. All the past work you have done under your birth
surname, including information found online, will still be connected to you if you keep your name. Clients can find you.

The more a person is along in their career, the less likely they
are to change their name. One woman said, *"I was already a
published writer with a career underway when I got married. I
didn't want the old me to disappear or colleagues and former students not to find me. It was important for my profession to keep*

my byline the same as it was before marriage. I didn't want to be punished for getting married. My husband didn't have to change anything or miss a beat."

- **Similar occupations as their spouse.** If you and your spouse are in the same or related occupations, clients/customers won't know you are married. This can keep it separate and professional. This is common practice with couples in many shared occupations such as acting, medicine, journalism, politics, etc.

- **Impact on income.** According to "Investopedia" (2019), women who keep their names earn more over the course of their careers. A 2010 University of Tilburg study found that women who keep their names earn $500,000 more over a lifetime than those who change their names to their husbands' names. Women who keep their names are viewed by those who hire as more ambitious and committed to work.

6. **Passing Along the Family Name**

- **Both family names passed along.** If each person in the couple retains their surnames, it keeps the continuity of both family names alive (not just one family name).

- **Last in line with the family name.** If the person (or couple) is the last member of their family with that surname, they may want each person's name to continue. Some feel a strong connection to their family name and history and want to continue the family name.

7. **Personal Advantages**

- **Honors both parents.** Keeping the birth surname honors the person's mother and father and their heritage and ethnicity.

- **Connection with friends**. Friends can find you more easily when your name remains the same for life.

- **Flexibility.** There may even be some advantages with food if you and your spouse are invited to a potluck dinner and asked to bring a dish according to the first letter of your last name. For instance, if A-L brings a salad, M-R brings an entrée, and S-Z brings a dessert, which last name do you use? This gives you the option to choose the one you want. I say, always err on the side of dessert!

- **Safety and security.** If one partner is a public figure, it can be helpful for safety and security to have two different last names. One person can "hide" more easily under the other person and his/her name if needed (e.g., from media, stalkers) and maintain more privacy and anonymity.

- **Bank accounts, utilities, and policies.** Most businesses are used to married couples having different last names when they help you open an account, buy property, or get an insurance policy. They cannot legally discriminate against you if you keep your last name, as was the case in the past. Rarely does anyone blink an eye these days. And, so what if they do? You may need to take an extra 15 seconds to state you each kept your names when you married. Frankly, I think it is fun to acquaint people with a practice about which they may have never thought.

- **Travel.** Some people fear they will experience difficulty traveling with their spouse in a foreign country if they have different last names. I have traveled to 40 countries, and no one has ever asked if my husband and I were married even with different last names on our passports and reservations. It has never been a problem. Additionally, many countries (some you might describe as conservative) do not have the tradition of women changing their names at marriage. In much of the world, married couples have different last names. If you are still concerned, carry a photocopy of your marriage license in your wallet.

Challenges of Name Option #1

1. Judgment by Others

- **Questioning your motive.** You may fear the judgment of others if you keep your surname. You may wonder if people will think you are less dedicated to the relationship or selfish rather than other-interested (e.g., you put your identity ahead of the man's). Some women feel they face a moral dilemma, choosing between their own self-interests and identity and that of the family.

  Women I interviewed who had kept their names said they had *no or very few comments* made to them through the years. However, some of the more memorable ones have included, *"What does your husband think of this?"* or *"This is disrespectful to your husband."* According to one woman, there was a period that some feared being labeled "feminist" like it was awful and evil. Another woman I interviewed, who was married in 2010, was forewarned by a woman in her church that she knew of a man who had an affair due to his resentment of his wife not taking his name. Interesting. I think there may have been more to that story...

As one woman said, I was worried my in-laws would care that I kept my name. They didn't care!

Several years ago, a man said to me in an inquisitive and slightly judgmental way, *"So, you didn't take your husband's name?"* and I responded, *"That's right. He didn't think I had earned it."* My comment was intended to be humorous and successfully stop the inquiry from going further. He was perplexed. Mission accomplished.

- **Viewed by others as competitive.** Some women who keep their names express concern over being viewed as "competitive" and not a team player in the marriage. With that logic, I would ask, is the *man* not a team player if he doesn't take *your* name? And, who would make this kind of judgmental statement to you in the first place? They probably don't know you very well. Plus, this says much more about that person's relationship, worldview regarding gender, and values than it does about yours. Additionally, there is a perception that a husband might feel emasculated or kidded by his friends if his wife keeps her birth surname (this concern does not seem to surface in same-sex relationships). Men I talked to whose wives kept their names said it is not an issue.

- **Wives who kept their names are held to a higher standard.** A 2017 study found that some people hold women with non-traditional surnames to a higher standard of "performance" as wives. For example, there are higher expectations of her being a good wife in the traditional sense (dutiful, cooks, cleans, pleasant, taking care of others' needs, etc.). Men who maintained their birth surnames did not experience a comparable gender role standard or expectation.

- **Viewed by others as less committed.** A small proportion of the population believes women who keep their names are not fully into the marriage and being married. A 2016 Portland State University study looked at 1,242 people nationwide and found that men, whose education did not go beyond high school, saw women who kept their maiden names as less dedicated to the marriage. They expressed that women could justifiably be divorced more easily if they kept their names. In the same study, women and men with higher education, did not share this view. They disagreed there was any connection between women's names and marital commitment. One woman said, *"I did not need to change my name to show my love and the depth of my commitment."*

A University of Nevada study in 2016 found that people with high or hostile sexism respond negatively to women who violate "traditional" gender roles, including names.

In Hillary Clinton's autobiography *Living History*, she recalled her mother and mother-in-law discouraging her from keeping her birth surname. Hillary was a lawyer, lecturer, author of numerous published articles, all under the name Hillary Rodham. It seemed more practical to her to keep her name when she got married. The social/political pressure became so great she added Clinton to the end of her name and became Hillary Rodham Clinton. Eventually, she was simply referred to as Hillary Clinton. In the mid-1990s, keeping her last name, even as a middle name, was a big issue and critically panned in the media. Some blamed Bill Clinton's loss for Governor of Arkansas on his wife using her birth surname.

Fast forward to now. Many married political couples have completely separate last names. Having different surnames has become a non-issue.

2. **Children**

- **How to name the kids.** Some people prefer to have all family members share the same last name. One woman said she felt "guilt" that she had a different last name from her child's last name. With option 1, children are often given one parent's last name as the child's middle name and the other parent's last name as the child's last name. That way, both the maternal and paternal family names are retained and passed along through the children, and the family unit is inter-connected through both parent's names. (See Chapter 10 on children naming options.)

- **Dilemma.** People who do not change their surname feel they were put in an arbitrary and perhaps antiquated conundrum of choosing between themselves and their family. In some social circles, a subtle message is conveyed that women (more so than men) should put family or future family first. Some believe deleting a woman's name is a selfless act she alone must undertake for a family to be created.

3. **Logistics**

- **Whose name to use.** There are very few logistical problems for couples who retain their birth surnames. The biggest one I have encountered is when making a dinner reservation at a restaurant. I would occasionally forget under which name I made the reservation. Voila! We now have a solution and use the name "Donner." Okay, it is kind of gallows humor when the maître 'd calls out our name, "Donner Party?" (We have also been known to use the last names "Beach" or "Toga," you know, any name that works well with the word "party" behind it.)

- **Assumptions by others.** Some people assume you have the same last name if you are married. Since that is the default assumption for some people, my husband has been called "Mr. Morgan," and I have been called "Mrs. Jordan." It is not a regular occurrence, and the world is still turning. One woman shared that she'd received a check one time written to her but using her husband's last name. The person had assumed that was her last name as well. She was still able to cash it.

- **Honorifics.** Although there is no consensus on this matter, the honorific "Mrs." doesn't exactly work well for a woman who retains her birth surname. That might be her mother, right? Many people assume a woman is married when she reaches a certain age, so they use "Mrs". when addressing her. Just a heads-up to those assumption-ers, about 30% of adult women have never married (up from 23% in 1990). Additionally, many feel that the marriage-neutral "Ms." is the better choice since it is the equivalent of "Mr." Using "Mr." or "Ms." or no honorific at all seems to work best when you retain your birth surname.

Since we are on the topic of honorifics, "Mrs." is derived from the title "mistress." The abbreviation was originally pronounced "mistress" (rather than pronounced "misses" as it is today). In the mid-18th century, mistress referred to a woman of social status and wealth or those who governed servants. Originally, it had nothing to do with the fact she was or wasn't married or anything about her sexual proclivities. It was simply a reference to the fact she was the female equivalent of "master."

"Miss" also came from the root word "mistress." It became a popular title in the 18th century, referring to an unmarried woman of status, usually a school teacher. It slowly began referring to young girls, while "master" was the title for young boys. By the late 18th century, the change in the "Miss" definition caused "Mrs." to change too, now meaning a married woman.

The folklore around the origin of Mr. and Mrs. focuses on the husband-wife owner relationship, covered in Chapter 3. The man was known as the master with the abbreviation "Mr." The honorific "Mr's" was put before the wife's name. It was short for master with an apostrophe put before the "s" indicating a possessive. That is, she was the property of the master. Through the years, the apostrophe was dropped and shortened to simply "Mrs." Although an interesting story and certainly consistent with the history of marriage laws, I was unable to unearth the origin of this explanation of Mr. and Mrs.

The first reference to the title "Ms." was in England in 1698. It was used for an unmarried woman or if her marital status was unknown. "Ms." is not a new concept, gaining traction in the United States in the 1970s during the second wave of feminism and the popularity of MS. Magazine. "Mrs." is used less widely today because of a more relaxed society as well as the increasingly popular title "Ms."

Many married lesbian couples today do not use the "Mrs." honorific. Some also avoid the term "wife" since it connotes a woman's deference to a man in straight culture.

4. Values

- **Conflict, confusion, or not.** Some argue that when a woman retains her birth surname, it is just using another man's name (her father's), so why not take her husband's name? For some people, this matters. For others, it is the fact that her surname was *her* surname since birth. The practice of keeping the last name is not denouncing all men. For most, it is a matter of maintaining one's identity and adhering to egalitarian marriage practices.

Examples of Name Option #1

(Before marriage) Jane Smith and John Jones
(After marriage) Jane Smith and John Jones

(Before marriage) Jason Darnell and Daveed Romain
(After marriage) Jason Darnell and Daveed Romain

Reviews of Name Option #1

Positive Reviews
In the marriages I have admired over the years, the woman kept her own name. That has always stuck with me.

I recognize all the effort and pain that came out of the women's movement. I want to thank them for their hard work so I could keep my own name.

When I kept my own name, I was not rejecting my husband. I was simply not rejecting myself.

I was married for 13 years to an emotionally abusive military man. He died by suicide, which was traumatic for me and my two small children. We all three changed our last names back to my maiden name as a fresh start.

Losing my name and taking his name perpetuates the gendered power hierarchy in marriage.

My Mom kept her maiden name when she married my Dad. It wasn't a big deal in our household.

Keeping my name was not a political statement. It was simple. I just wanted my name. It belonged to me.

I don't have any female friends or family who have taken their husband's last name. It seems strange to me that people still say this practice is the exception!

I'm married and kept my last name. I think it makes some people uncomfortable. Good.

Using his name represents a time when men had absolute power over women. Women were subsumed by men and the names showed it. All women should know this before they choose to take their husband's name.

I kept my name in marriage. I have no regrets and am still proud of that decision. My husband is too. Neither of us wanted me to become "Mrs. His Name." I'm surprised when young women don't even think about keeping their name or other options.

I did not want to be defined as "wife of" anyone and preferred to be seen as me, married to a wonderful man. Using "Mrs." seems to be fading (oddly, schools and country clubs seem to hang onto this anti-quated practice). It never worked for me.

Why rush off and legally change all their ID as an homage to paternalism?

My daughter kept her maiden name, but most of her friends did not. It is a strange and disappointing nod to male chauvinism.

I kept my name, and he kept his. Nothing exploded, no one died. All is good.

We have never had a problem with our names. If anyone called and asked for "Mrs. His Last Name", I gave them my mother-in-law's phone number.

When my wife and I got married (we are gay), it didn't even occur to us to change our names. Why would we? Our names are part of our family histories. It seems so very old fashioned to change names, and not in a cute, quaint way.

A person's last name has nothing to do with their love. You show love through deeds, not names.

I wasn't willing to change my name, so I couldn't ask my wife to change hers. Why would she? It is indefensible.

I feel very fortunate. I found a partner who makes me feel worthy and empowered and is secure enough to break with the married name tradition.

I don't think marrying someone makes my past accomplishments ir-relevant. I put a lot of energy into creating a reputation using my name and brand. Why erase that? I am proud of who I've become. He gets it. He is proud of me, too.

My words and actions are the measures of my love and commitment to my partner. My last name has nothing to do with marital success.

My husband honors my independence and never asked me to change my name.

I felt it was scary to change my name, and why would I? So, I never did.

I have been tracing our family tree. My maternal and paternal sides are equal (50-50 DNA), yet the whole genealogy thing is very male-centric. I can find my father's side but it is much harder to trace my mother's side because of names. There is such a focus on "carrying the family name," yet the family name favors the man's name.

Growing up, I heard, "you can do and be anything you want. You don't need a man to do it for you." That was juxtaposed with the culture telling me "a charming prince will rescue you and take care of you." Young people don't need to hear any more fairytale fantasies.

Throughout my childhood, I saw my mother introduce, sign, and think of herself as "Mrs. Harold Jackson." It was a matter of pride for her to adopt my father's entire name (first and last) and stop using her own. I loved my parents, but I decided early-on that I would never give up my own identity.

Since no man has to explain why he kept his name, it seems reasonable that I shouldn't either.

Negative Reviews

If you have children, you are more likely to have strangers (mostly school and medical settings) call you by your children's last name even if your name is different. People make assumptions.

I kept my maiden name, and we still get mail from our family (not our friends) as "Mr. and Mrs. my-husband's-name." I have no idea why my mother-in-law cannot bring herself to write my real name.

Some people in town thought my brother was my husband since we had the same last name.

Since my husband and son had a different last name from mine, I felt like I was not wearing the team jersey.

Notes on Option #1:

CHAPTER 5

NAME OPTION #2:
TAKE YOUR SPOUSE'S LAST NAME AND ELIMINATE YOUR LAST NAME

Description of Name Option #2

In Option #2, one spouse's last name is used as the family name. With this surname sharing option, either person's last name can be used, although in heterosexual marriages, the man's last name is typically the one retained for the couple, and the woman's last name is eliminated.

Taking one spouse's name is often referred to as being "traditional," however it is not considered traditional in many countries and cultures, nor is it a universal practice in the United States. Yet, it is the most popular option in the United States and the United Kingdom. It's estimated that about 70-80% of married women choose this option. Statistics are not available for same-sex couples. People who chose to eliminate their surname in favor of the other person's surname generally do so because of family concerns such as children, showing family connection and solidarity, marital union and commitment, avoiding confusion, disassociating from the family of origin, appeasing his/her future spouse, and a desire for creating a whole new family.

For the same reasons a woman changes her last name, it is reasonable to assume that men would consider this option. Yet, only a small number of men (about 3%) change their last name at marriage. Research suggests that option #2 male-focused name privilege is more gratifying to men than women. Many women who change their names state that this gesture symbolizes their union, yet few men share these sentiments about changing their own names. Less than half of the people in a 2013 study said that a man should even be *allowed* to take his wife's last name. That same year, a Florida man successfully forced the DMV to accept his decision to take his wife's last name. When musician Jack White was married to Meg White, he took her last name. They later divorced but he kept her last name for professional reasons. In 2007, California passed the "Name Equality Act" that allows either spouse to change his/her name at marriage, using the marriage license as the means to change.

It is interesting to note that as of this writing, only eight states allow men to change their names at the point of marriage or divorce in the same way women can do. Men can certainly change their names. However, most states require it to be done as a separate court filing process (and expense). It is not the simple name form to complete that accompanies the marriage license. This is certainly discrimination against men and will no doubt be changed in the coming years, especially since same-sex marriage is now legal. This also impacts a man who wants to adopt his wife's last name or hyphenate their names together. The upshot is that men and same-sex male couples should be able to change their names the same way women are allowed to do in heterosexual marriages. Name change done at the time of marriage should be gender-neutral. Stay tuned.

In same-sex marriages, couples may decide to use one partner's last name and eliminate the other's last name for the sake of having one family name. Although anecdotal data is now starting to emerge, it appears that many married same-sex couples do not change their names at all. Most retain their birth surnames.

Some celebrities have chosen to take their spouse's last name and drop their own name: Victoria Adams ("Posh Spice") married David Beckham and became Victoria Beckham; Amal Alamuddin married George Clooney and became Amal Clooney; Hailey Baldwin married Justin Bieber and became Hailey Bieber; Presidential candidate "Mayor Pete" Buttigieg's husband Chasten Glezman changed his last name and is now Chasten Buttigieg.

Benefits of Name Option #2

1.   Family Unity/One Name/Children

- **Family name.** The primary reason one person takes the other's last name is about family. They want to share a common name. This gesture shows unity, solidarity, commitment, and being a "team." You are more easily identified as a married couple and family. One person said, *"It is like a tattoo. Permanent."*

- **Same name as children.** It labels the family together and connects the parent and child. It avoids any problems or confusion a parent may have using a different last name. Additionally, many women see giving up their names as the quid pro quo required to create a family.

- **An outward sign of union.** It is an outward sign of a union. It can deepen the bond.

2. Romantic

- **Act of love.** A woman changing her last name to her husband's name is viewed as "romantic" and an act of love. One woman said, *"I was madly in love with him and wanted to identify with him through my name."* Another woman said, *"I didn't want to give up my name, but I did as a sacrifice to him."*

3. Pleases Spouse, Family

- **It makes others happy.** Older family members or your spouse's family may be happy about your decision to change your name (if they are female relatives, they probably had to change their names) and may not understand or know about other name options.

- **Path of least resistance.** Not "rocking the boat" may reduce pressure or conflict from others. You may feel safe and comfortable in doing the familiar.

4. Tradition

- **Connection.** Women taking their husbands' names and eliminating their own can be viewed as a tradition all women experience.

- **Conformity.** I had a friend who got married and moved to a small town where she was a school teacher. She took her husband's last name because she was concerned the community would wonder if she was really married or just "living in sin," as they used to say. Teachers were often viewed as moral role models in society. She was concerned about her job and what the neighbors or the postal carrier might think if she and her husband had different last names. Those issues are fading from our cultural lexicon but may still be an issue in more conservative parts of the country.

What your friends and family do with their own names can impact your decision about names. What you see around you can create a subtle social/peer pressure to conform.

5. Religion

- **Gender roles.** Some change their last names for religious reasons, originating from teachings on gender roles in marriage. Some see women taking their husbands' names as an extension of their husband-wife roles (see Chapter 2 on Religion).

6. Better Name

- **Easier name.** Some people take their spouse's last name because it is better than their own name. The spouse's last name may be easier to spell, pronounce, or simply sound better. It may be less embarrassing or have a derogatory double-meaning. It feels more like an upgrade to change the name. One woman shared that she had a long, ethnic surname she was ready to change. *"I felt different from other kids growing up. I have always wanted to blend in and be accepted. Now I can."*

Another woman shared that taking her husband's name was an easy choice. His last name was common, and her name was hard to pronounce and spell. *"I'm still me, with my beliefs about feminism and women's roles in marriage and in the world, but now I don't have to correct people about my name."*

- **More American name.** Some take their partner's last name because it sounds more American, allowing them to feel like they fit in better. Having a Mexican last name, one woman said she was subjected to derogatory comments and racist remarks. She wanted to avoid that discomfort. She was given her father's last name, despite not being raised by him. She said the name meant nothing to her, and couldn't wait to change it for these two reasons.

- **Prestigious name.** Sometimes the spouse's name is more prestigious (money, power, fame, reputation). For example, if a woman is marrying into a prominent, well-known family, the name has caché. It could open up doors in business, politics, and social settings.

7. Disassociate from Family of Origin/Negative Past

- **Cut ties to family.** A new name can indicate a rejection of ties with your family of origin and hence, your family name. Some wish to change their names to disassociate from their family where abuse or trauma occurred. Some feel that their last name was really their father's last name anyway, not theirs. There are many reasons why people want to cut ties with the past.

  One woman said, *"I couldn't drop my last name fast enough. I had a horrible, rocky, and unstable childhood. A new name felt like a fresh start."*

- **Erase identity.** Some people wish to escape from the law, a stalker, or an unfortunate past relationship. One way to help with that process is through a name change.

8. **Show of Love and Commitment**

- **Consistent with values.** Changing your last name to your spouse's may be consistent with your value system. Changing your name is a way to show your love by giving up something of value. One woman said, *"giving up my name felt like the ultimate gift I could do for my husband. I felt great pride."*

- **Start to a new life.** Many brides- and grooms-to-be are excited to start a new life together. A name signifies the start of a new chapter as a couple and family. Unquestionably, there is strength and influence in a name change. For example, if you are a transgender female and changed your name from Bradley to Serina, the new name may feel more genuine and authentic. If you divorce and go back to your birth surname, you may feel empowered that you reclaimed (a verb I often heard in my interviews) your name. You have been dating long distance for years. You finally get married and are together in one place with one name. Name changes impact how you see your world, inwardly and outwardly, and how it sees you.

  One woman stated, *"I didn't feel married until I took his name."*

9. **External Declaration of Being Married/Change in Status/ Identity**

- **Announcing new status.** You are now married, not single. Changing your last name is a way to let others know of your new status and that you are now off the market. You embrace your new identity, and the name is a reflection of that.

Challenges of Name Option #2

1. Time Consuming, Cost, Hassle

- **Time.** It can be time-consuming and a hassle to change your name and all the records/legal documents associated with it (see Chapter 12 for a list of places). Some changes may include a fee. In this electronic day and age, even changing an email address that contains your birth last name can be a hassle. People who change their names also have a greater chance of encountering problems with things accumulated or earned under their birth surname (e.g., credit they have established, frequent flyer points).

2. One Partner's Loss of Identity/Heritage

- **Only one family name continues.** This option only keeps one person's family name alive. The person giving up his/her name does not keep their family name going.

- **Name/identity subsumed.** The person changing his/her name may feel subsumed by the other partner (see Chapter 3 discussion on Coverture, identity). Some people stated they felt *submerged* rather than *merged* when their own name disappeared. The concept of mutual, two-way solidarity may not be present when one person's name goes away.

  In spite of what many women think, one woman said you do lose a part of who you are if you change your name. People start asking you, *"who were you before?"* That is how they phrase it. Keeping your own name in some form is a reminder of who you are, where you came from, and who you are now.

- **Loss of ethnicity and heritage.** Some people experience a loss of ethnic and cultural connection when a birth surname is given up. Sunny Hostin, author, and actress on *The View*, said she would not have ever changed her name if she had to do it over again. Her family name was Asuncion and difficult for people to pronounce. Being Puerto Rican, Jewish, and African American, she felt like she disregarded herself when she changed her name. One woman shared similar comments, *"I felt like I lost my ethnicity. I had a Jewish last name, and now I don't."*

- **Regret.** Some women have expressed regret at giving up their names and identity. Even if you are excited about being married, the "old you" disappears.

3. Goes Against Values

- **Sexist/imbalance of power.** Changing the last name for a woman can carry a message that she values a particular marital hierarchy. A woman eliminating her name and taking the man's name is "the last socially-acceptable sexism", says sociologist Laurie Scheuble. Not allowing women to join or fully participate in clubs and organizations is seen as wrong and discriminatory. Paying women less money than men for equal work is also seen as unfair and illegal. That said, why do the majority of couples in the United States continue to give men's surnames preference over women's surnames?

4. Personal Losses

- **Hard to find.** There may be lost opportunities personally (e.g., old friends and colleagues may have more difficulty finding you).

5. Professional Losses

- **Starting over.** There may be lost opportunities professionally. When a person changes his/her name, there is the risk of rebuilding a career and reputation. It may be hard, and take time, to reestablish yourself with a different last name.

6. Fairness/Loss of Power/Respect

- **Being fair.** It can feel unfair and one-sided when one spouse (usually the man) does not change his name.

- **Limited options.** Some say women give into taking their husbands' name because there is no good alternative, especially if they plan to have children. (See Chapter 10 for children naming suggestions)

Examples of Name Option #2

(Before marriage) Jane Smith and John Jones
(After marriage) Jane Jones and John Jones (or) Jane Smith and John Smith

(Before marriage) Jason Darnell and Daveed Romain
(After marriage) Jason Romain and Daveed Romain (or) Jason Darnell and Daveed Darnell

Reviews of Name Option #2

Positive Reviews
We are now a team, and I wanted a team name.

I always wanted to be a wife and mother. I was proud to take his name so we could start our family. My husband loves and protects me. I wanted to honor him and our marriage in this way.

My name shows I have a new family now. I want people to know I am married to him and he is married to me. It is a symbol of solidarity. Families feel closer when they all share a last name.

My grandparents came to the US from Italy. My grandmother kept her surname when they married (the law in Italy). On their way across the ocean on a ship, she had to change her last name to his because that was the law in the US. She gladly did so because they were thrilled to come to America to live.

The wife should take the last name of the husband, as he is the head of the family. Sharing a last name is our Christian belief.

There is something romantic and old-fashioned about giving up your name.

I vowed to be his wife and bear his children. I vowed to put him above everyone, including my parents. Deleting my name and using his, symbolized the significance of that commitment.

Trying to change a woman's role (raising family, keeping husband happy) invites societal disruption and family unhappiness. Taking his name should be her greatest honor.

I have no regrets changing my name to my husband's. But I quietly hope my daughters will keep their names.

I was excited to become Mrs. Richard MacKenzie. But was I excited about being married or being Mrs. his name not mine? Those are two different things.

I happily gave up my last name. It was a chance to separate from an unhappy childhood name.

I'm happily married and don't care what people call me. I know who I am and so does my husband.

Some women view taking their husband's name as a strategic move. This was especially true when women had no power, could not make their own way in the world, and were denied opportunities.

Taking my husband's name was an easy choice. My father never paid child support and had abandoned us. Women who keep their maiden names must love and respect their fathers – I envy that relationship.

Stay beneath your husband's umbrella.

I took my husband's last name to be a family unit. I was broken, now I am whole. I was never happy and now life is love-filled.

My grandfather passed away years ago. Yet, my grandmother still takes incredible pride in being Mrs. His Name.

I kept my maiden name but later changed it because I felt guilty that my name didn't match the people I love.

I took his name as a symbol of our lives fusing together as one. A name is the glue that holds us together.

It was important to my husband that I take his name. It was also important to my mother who had changed her name when she married.

I changed my name to show I was serious about the marriage.

It felt like the right thing to do. I can't explain why.

Negative Reviews

The thing that makes you an appendage of the male is the substitution of his first and last name for yours.

We need to stop sleepwalking into an outdated, sexist practice that does us, and our daughters, no good.

I said 'I do' and was blissfully happy. Until I wasn't. I loved being married yet there was a persistent undercurrent of loss. I felt I had lost myself and disappeared somewhere along the way. There is no question I adore my husband but who am I now? Where did I go? No one talked to me about the fact I had a choice about my married last name. I was caught up in the whirlwind of the wedding and the romance of it all. I spent more time selecting wedding cake frosting with flowers that matched my bouquet than thinking about my name.

I was oblivious to what my name meant to me or that it was even important. I've since learned there are many ways people show they are a couple. What I had decided to do with my name (take his) I realize now was not a good fit for me —my personal and professional life, identity and joy.

Taking his name felt like wearing a sweater that didn't fit. It was too tight and I felt uncomfortable.

Changing my name paved the way for our future. Although, it made me sad to say goodbye to my name.

I have some old cookbooks compiled by women in the 1960s. The recipes list the credits as "Mrs. (husband's first and last name)." He essentially gets the credit. You have no idea who these women are.

Everyone knew me by my former name. The first year of marriage, every time we got mail to "Mr. and Mrs." I cried.

Taking your husband's last name can feel like you are betraying your politics and values. It is misogynistic.

I love my husband but it feels like I am piggy-backing on his life.

I told my future husband I would take his name. That night, I laid awake for hours grieving that loss of my last name. It still plagues me.

Automatically taking the husband's last name is normalizing male supremacy. Can't the husband and wife be valued equally (by taking either name or no new name) and still achieve family cohesion?

A friend returning from her honeymoon sent out a text, "Rest in Peace (her maiden name)" It felt so hostile to her old self. She had to kill it?

When you take your husband's name, expect lots of paperwork for years.

If this is a second marriage, you have to ask yourself if you are going to change your name again to your new husband's name. Why keep changing identities?

Name changing is a symbolic gesture that sends a message about who has power. He does nothing and retains everything he has always had, including his name and all that goes with it.

What a hassle. When I changed my last name, I lost all of my airline frequent flyer points. I am still trying to get this mess straightened out.

Why do women blindly follow tradition when the tradition has a bad history, doesn't benefit them and sends a message of giving away power and selfhood?

I was eager to change my name and dutifully did the tedious steps to make that happen. Why didn't I think I could be all these things – loyal partner, devoted wife – without giving up my name?

I believed taking his name was something a wife does so her husband doesn't feel slighted. I didn't want him to feel bad and I worried what others would think. Why is it that some think a woman who keeps her name 'weakens' her husband but when a man keeps his name, it doesn't reflect on her?

Changing my last name has continued to haunt my records and personal finances. It was a nightmare changing everything.

Knowing the history of married last names, are these naming traditions worth continuing? It still feels like women are "less than" and still treated as property. Simply because it's "what we've always done" is demeaning to everyone.

I'm white and my husband is Asian. I took his name and have been overlooked in places because people keep looking for an Asian woman rather than calling out my name.

After I got married, people at work would ask me, 'Who did you used to be before you got married?' Used to be? It feels like the old me is gone along with the name.

The name change was more emotional than I thought it would be and a little painful. I miss my old name.

I feel like I lost an outward symbol of my ethnic heritage when I gave up my Greek name.

I associate my new surname with my husband's relatives, whom I dislike.

When I got married, I took my husband's last name because of future children but I didn't like the way our last names sounded together. If I could do it over again, I would hyphenate.

Marrying someone does not mean I want to become him.

Sadly, my family's surname will die with me.

I was horrified when my mother showed me my birth announcement which read "Mr. and Mrs. Eric Lewis announce...." My mother had done all the work for nine months and many years to follow, so where was her name? I told her it should read "Susan Lewis and sperm donor announce..."

We spent months of planning for the wedding and honeymoon. But no one emotionally prepared me for the name change. We said I do and the minister declared to the attendees that we were now Mr. and Mrs. Jason Walters. But where did Ashley go? Not only that, where did Ashley Morrison go? Both of my names just evaporated. He was and still is Jason Walters.

Notes on Option #2:

CHAPTER 6

NAME OPTION #3: USE YOUR BIRTH SURNAME AS YOUR MIDDLE NAME AND ADD YOUR PARTNER'S SURNAME AS YOUR LAST NAME

Description of Name Option #3

This is a popular married name option, also called "maiden to middle," that uses one person's surname as a middle name and the other person's surname as the last name. This naming option eliminates the existing middle name (usually the bride's or it can be both partners) in order to plug in her birth surname into that middle spot, then add the spouse's surname to the end. Some people find this a balance between taking your spouse's name and keeping your own name.

Often in heterosexual couples, the woman is the only one who changes her name in this way, so Helena Mason Watson would put her birth surname Mason as her new middle name and add Watson, her husband's last name, as her new last name. However, both couples may choose to use each other's surnames as their middle names and keep their birth surname as their last name. Some opt to do the surnames in various middle and last name combinations (see examples below).

According to Southern Weddings Magazine, this "maiden to middle" naming tradition has southern roots. Some girls in the south are not given middle names at birth (estimated around 20%) to simplify the process of sliding her surname into the middle name slot when she marries. They are taught at a young age that they will be deleting their *middle* name when they marry. This is a different message from what other girls hear: they will be deleting their last name when they marry.

One of the most famous couples who took each other's last names and used them as middle names was John Ono Lennon and Yoko Ono Lennon. Other known people to take their birth last name and use it as a middle name then add their husband's name (but their husbands did not make this change) include Ruth Bader Ginsberg, Doris Kerns Goodwin, Hillary Rodham Clinton, Kim Kardashian West, Jenna Bush Hager, Coretta Scott King, Candace Cameron Bure, Salma Hayek Pinault, and Christy Turlington Burns.

Benefits of Name Option #3

1. **Retains Birth Surname While Incorporating New Married Surname**

- **Incorporates both partner's names.** Both names go forward in the family tree and lineage. It is an outward display of valuing each name equally. If both people in the couple decide to use both surnames (in the middle and last name slots), each person retain their birth surname. For instance, if David Taylor married Ashton Cuomo, they would become David Taylor Cuomo and Ashton Taylor Cuomo. The couple needs to decide which name becomes the new middle name and which become the new last name. Some sequence the names in alphabetical order, some by preference to how it sounds, and some by who feels the strongest about being in which order. Sometimes they are not in the same order.

2. Helps with Professional Continuity

- **Not starting over.** This option helps with continuity in professional life (networking, past clients, publishing) since your surname is not entirely eliminated after marriage. People may still be able to recognize you and make the name connection for career continuity.

- **Credit for past work.** You are less likely to lose the connection with your past work and credits under your birth name. Helps with professional continuity since birth surname is included in married person's name, making the connection with past professional work.

- **Others can find you.** It is easier for others to find you professionally if the birth surname is not completely dropped.

3. Helps with Personal Continuity, Identity

- **It shows you are married.** It allows you to keep your name and identity but shows you are married.

- **Maintain identity.** If you are sentimental and closely aligned with your name yet want to add your spouse's name to yours, this may be a good option. You are less likely to have an identity issue because you are hanging onto your name, a familiar part of you.

- **Children have names from both parents.** This is a good option for those who want to maintain their own identity and are also concerned about future children having different last names from their parents. (See Chapter 10 on children's names)

- **Reduces records problems.** Having your original surname as your middle name can make it easier to verify who you are if there is ever a problem with records, accounts, credit, etc.

- **Honors past and family.** Moving your surname into your middle name slot is a great way to honor your past while honoring your commitment to your new partner and future with him/her. You take on your new name while keeping the old name. This can be a good compromise.

4.   Creates a Common Family Name

- **Same last name.** The couple shares a common family name. It connects the couple and children together.

Challenges to Name Option #3

1.   Time Consuming and Hassle

- **Change all records.** You will have to change all records as you would with any name change (time-consuming, hassle, costs, the potential for problems, etc.)

- **State laws.** As of this writing, a handful of states do not allow people to change their middle name at the time of marriage, only their last name. In those states, middle name changes need to go through a separate court process, whether you are a man or a woman. Check with the local county clerk where you are getting married to be sure you are doing what needs to occur legally for this kind of name change. Everything from your driver's license to passport must be the exact same name. As a response to terrorism, the United States government in recent years has increased the number of documents needed to verify who you are and have clamped down on inconsistency. After many years of marriage and using their birth surname as their middle name, some people have discovered that their state did not "recognize" the middle name change and had to go through a court process to rectify the discrepancy. Likewise, signing your ballot when voting must match up exactly, or your vote may not count.

2. **Loss of Middle Name**

- **Sadness around loss.** In the United States, approximately three out of four people have middle names. Some people drop their birth middle name so that their birth surname becomes the new legal middle name. This option can be difficult for those not wanting to give up their middle names. Middle names often have special significance, such as the name of a beloved relative. For some, deleting that name can feel uncomfortable and unfair, bringing a sense of loss and sadness. Some people try to keep all four names, sometimes having two middle names or two last names. However, this approach can get cumbersome.

  One woman told me, *"I loved my middle name Amisha. I was named after my Aunt. Sadly, I had to legally drop Amisha as it was replaced by my maiden name when I added my husband's name to the end of my name."* Several others expressed grief at losing their original middle names to make this option work.

  Some people are unclear if their birth last name should be part of the married last name (just sitting in front or behind the new last name so there are two last names) or a second middle name (sitting in front or behind the existing middle name so there are two middle names). If the birth middle name is deleted, this double middle name or double last name issue may not be a concern. Having four names can get confusing on forms.

- **The name is dropped.** Over time, many people say they stop using their new middle name (their birth surname) and just use their new last name (the spouse's surname).

3. Need to Educate and Correct Others

- **Explaining name.** It may take a little education to let others know your name preference.

- **Family concerns.** Your relatives (and friends) might have a problem with you giving up your birth surname. Families feel pride in a name that reflects their heritage, ethnicity, and culture. It can run deep, and giving up your name can feel like abandoning where you came from. You may need to take time to explain it isn't eliminated but moved in order – it is now in the middle.

4. Goes Against Values

- **A burden on women.** It can feel like you are going against your value system because you are "taking his name" and not retaining your birth surname. It could build resentment if your partner did not change his name.

Examples of Name Option #3

(Before marriage) Jane Smith and John Jones
(After marriage) Jane Smith Jones and John Jones (or)
Jane Jones Smith and John Jones (or)
Jane Smith Jones and John Smith Jones (or)
Jane Jones Smith and John Jones Smith (or)
Jane Smith and John Smith Jones (or)
Jane Smith and John Jones Smith (or)
Jane Jones Smith and John Smith Jones

(Before marriage) Jason Darnell and Daveed Romain
(After marriage) Jason Darnell Romain and Daveed Romain (or)
Jason Darnell and Daveed Romain Darnell (or)
Jason Darnell Romain and Daveed Darnell Romain (or)
Jason Romain Darnell and Daveed Romain Darnell (or)
Jason Romain Darnell and Daveed Darnell Romain

Reviews of Name Option #3

Positive Reviews

I love my last name and use it in the middle, with my husband's last name as my last name. Our daughter has my last name as a middle name and his as her last name. It works!

I did not share a last name with my mother (who was married many times), my brother or step-father, only with my deadbeat Dad. So, I wanted to share a name with my children. My feminist friends told me I sold out, but I needed a tangible link to my kids.

I have both of my parents' last names (as a middle and last name). I think it honors both of them by keeping their names.

I have never regretted fusing our names together: my maiden name is now my middle name and I added him to the end.

Keeping my maiden name in the middle allowed me to feel like we were a family. We all shared a last name but I was not lost in the process. My name is still there.

Negative Reviews

I wanted to have two last names (mine and my husband's) without a hyphen. I was surprised that the form I filled out at the end of the wedding only had three spots for names: first, middle and last. Sadly, I had to drop my middle name of Belle. I was named after my grandmother. My maiden name became my middle name. Thinking about it now, I probably would have done something differently to try to figure out how to keep all four names.

Although I like having my name and his, it is too many names and a mouthful. I sound like a law firm.

Notes on Option #3:

CHAPTER 7

NAME OPTION #4: HYPHENATE THE TWO LAST NAMES

Description of Name Option #4

In this option, the two last names of the couple are hyphenated together also referred to as a "double-barreled" last name. One person in the couple can make this change (e.g., most frequently the woman in heterosexual marriages) or both people. It is an individual preference which of the two last names goes first in the hyphenated combination. However, in heterosexual marriages, the woman's last name is often placed before the man's name. It is estimated that about 6% of brides in the United States hyphenate their last names. It is unknown how many men or same-sex couples hyphenate their names.

Beyonce and Jay-Z may be the most well-known couple where both people hyphenated their last names together. His birth surname was Carter, and her birth surname was Knowles. Their legal married names are Shawn Knowles-Carter and Beyonce Knowles-Carter. To mix things up a little bit, Beyonce went on a worldwide concert tour in 2013 called "The Mrs. Carter Show."

When actor Lorenzo Lamas married Shawna Craig, he was the one who wanted to hyphenate their names together. His name became Lorenzo Lamas-Craig, and her name remained the same, Shawna Craig. Other well-known hyphenated last names include Jill Wine-Banks (Watergate prosecutor), Priyaka Chopra-Jonas (actress) and Jada Pinkett-Smith (actress).

Benefits of Name Option #4

1. **Retains Birth Surname While Incorporating New Married Last Name**

- **Both names are used.** This option incorporates both names into the married last name. Because one person's surname is not eliminated, it maintains that person's old and new identity.

- **Partnership.** It presents an image of a partnership and not one dominated by one person's name.

2. **Helps with Professional Continuity**

- **Not starting over.** It helps with continuity in professional life (networking, past clients, publishing) since your surname is not eliminated after marriage.

- **Credit for past work.** You are less likely to lose the connection with your past work and credits under your birth name. Helps with professional continuity since birth surname is included in married person's name, making the connection with past professional work.

3. **Helps with Personal Continuity**

- **Others can find you.** It is easier for friends and acquaintances to find you if the birth surname is not completely dropped.

4. **Creates a Connection to a "Family" Name**

- **New married life.** It announces that you are now married.

- **Connects to your new family and spouse.** Honors the union of both families and your roots.

Challenges of Name Option #4

1. **Awkward**

- **Cumbersome and long**. It takes time to write and say.

- **The need to spell.** Because people expect only one last name, you may have to spell it more often. You may also have to explain that it is a hyphenated name.

2. **Record and Paperwork Problems**

- **The name doesn't fit.** Some paper and online forms can't accommodate a hyphenated last name. It may not recognize the hyphen symbol and/or have enough space for the length of a long, hyphenated name. Since some computers don't understand words with hyphens, it may become necessary to drop the hyphen and run the two last names together to make it one name or just use one of the names for it to "work."

3. Time Consuming and Hassle

- **Change all records.** You will have to change all records as you would with any name change (time-consuming, costs, the potential for problems, etc.)

4. Full Name Not Used Correctly by Others

- **Too long.** Because the surname is long, some people drop the first or last surname in the hyphen, defeating the reason the two names were put together.

- **Forget the name order.** Some people forget and reverse the order of the two names.

5. Family Name Not Used by All

- **Usually, only one person hyphenates.** If only one person hyphenates the last names, that person still has a different last name than their partner and possibly children. Even if the mom hyphenates her last name, the kids often do not.

- **Only good for one generation.** Hyphenated names are only workable for one generation since you can't hyphenate the last names together forever. Even in one generation, which surname(s) do you give the kids?

- **You must be consistent.** You can't flip-flop the order of the names or simply start using only one of the two names.

- **Inconsistent alphabetizing.** You may find inconsistency in how you are listed or recorded with plane reservations, conference registrations, medical appointments, etc. If your last name is Block-Klein, are you listed under B or K?

Because of this B or K issue, one woman said she was turned down from getting credit. They said there was no credit history under that hyphenated name even though she tried to explain she had a good credit history under one of the names in the hyphen (the first name, her surname). Note: this has the potential to happen whenever a name is changed.

- **British aristocracies.** People familiar with the British class traditions may find hyphenated last names pretentious. However, these traditions are generally not known in the United States. If an English minor noble "married up", especially if marrying the line's heiress, he would hyphenate his name behind his wife's (e.g., Windsor-Mountbatten).

Examples of Name Option #4

(Before marriage) Jane Smith and John Jones
(After marriage) Jane Smith-Jones and John Jones (or)
Jane Smith and John Jones-Smith (or)
Jane Smith-Jones and John Smith-Jones (or)
Jane Jones-Smith and John Jones-Smith

(Before marriage) Jason Darnell and Daveed Romain
(After marriage) Jason Darnell-Romain and Daveed Romain (or)
Jason Darnell and Daveed Romain-Darnell (or)
Jason Darnell-Romain and Daveed Darnell-Romain (or)
Jason Romain-Darnell and Daveed Romain-Darnell

Reviews of Name Option #4

Positive Reviews

My husband and I each hyphenated our names. We are a unified front.

Hyphenating names shows we are equal partners and it challenges the status quo of marriage traditions.

I hyphenated my last name when I married and it sounds great phonetically.

I feel quite unique, special and fancy with a new long name.

We are two gay men and we decided we would both hyphenate our names. It made no sense if just one of us changed our name.

We wanted to set a good example for our little family going forward so both our names are used as one name.

It reflects that we are both heads of the household, we are valued equally. It is a display of our conscious decision to be a partnership and union.

I kept my maiden name when we married but after a while, I wanted more of a connection to my husband. So, I decided to hyphenate our names. I feel more like a couple now.

Negative Reviews

My first name is hyphenated, so hyphenating our two last names together was just way too much.

Hyphenated names seem to confuse people for some reason.

I had a hyphenated last name but it was awkward and I was constantly spelling it for people. I finally just dropped my maiden name (the first part of the hyphen) and now just use his last name.

My hyphenated name was too long, difficult to spell and took forever to write. I ended up just using my husband's last name after a few years.

Notes on Option #4:

CHAPTER 8

NAME OPTION #5:
CREATE NEW LAST NAME
FOR COUPLE

Description of Name Option #5

Some couples create a whole new family last name. It can be a new name, a borrowed name, or a hybrid creation. Some couples use a meaningful or symbolic word, a favorite location, something from nature, or the name of a city, such as where they met. It can be a fresh start for a couple who wishes to move forward with no historical or familial ties to the past.

Although it is legal to create a completely new last name, you may need to file a legal name change and go through that process. Your marriage certificate/papers may or may not provide a way to change it in that kind of way legally. You will want to check with an attorney on this one.

Actors Carlos PenaVega and Alexa PenaVega created a whole new last name with their combined names of Pena and Vega. The former mayor of Los Angeles, Antonio Villaraigosa, combined his last name Villar with his former wife's last name, Raigosa. A social activist couple legally changed their last names to Peace.

My mother would often refer to us as the MoJos (taking the first two initials of my last name *Mo*rgan and my husband's last name *Jo*rdan). MoJo is a fun shorthand and endearing nickname but not our legal name. An informal nickname is always an option if you want a unique name.

Benefits of Name Option #5

1.   Creates a Common Family Name

- **One family name.** Both partners share the same last name, so there is one family name, a unit/team.

- **Symbol of equality.** It is fair since no one person has to "give up" their name; both do. Both are sacrificing and giving up the same regarding names. More egalitarian view of the relationship since both partners change names.

2.   Fresh Start from the Past

- **New name.** A new name satisfies both partners who want a fresh start, a clean slate or a break from their families and past life.

- **Non-traditional.** In same-sex couples, it is a way to distance themselves from heteronormativity.

- **Meaningful name.** Some couples select names with historical, religious, ethnic, cultural, or symbolic significance. Some people change their name to honor someone important in their lives or combine two cultural heritages into one new word.

Challenges to Name Option #5

1. Both People Have to Change Records

- **Time-consuming, hassle, expense.** You both have to change all your legal records, accounts, etc., which can be time-consuming and incur costs.

- **Problems.** Possible confusion on legal or government records such as social security, etc., but probably no more than other last name changes.

2. Genealogy Issues

- **Family tree.** A new name out of the blue may drive genealogists up the family tree. In future years, those conducting this research may have a difficult time making connections with other relatives. Although this could be true with all name changes, this choice may create more problems for those who are tracking family ancestry since it may not connect to anyone else in the tree.

3. Personal Connections

- **Family.** This choice has the potential to offend, feel like a rejection, or hurt relatives' feelings in both families.

- **Friends.** It may be harder for old friends to find you and your spouse.

- **Identity concerns.** It has the potential for identity issues for the couple since each person gives up their birth names.

Examples of Name Option #5

(Before marriage) Jane Smith and John Jones
(After marriage) Jane Ceilo and John Ceilo

(Before marriage) Jason Darnell and Daveed Romain
(After marriage) Jason Domain and Daveed Domain

Reviews of Name Option #5

Positive Reviews
It gave us both a totally new, exciting fresh start.

I like that we have a common family name. And it is unique!

We put a lot of thought into our new name. It means a lot to us. We love it.

Our name reflects us because we chose it.

Negative Reviews
It was hard to get used to at first.

Some friends and family were confused as to why we took a whole new name but it worked for us.

Our new name was not a word you would hear as a last name, so I am always spelling and explaining it. Some people don't take me seriously.

Notes on Option #5:

CHAPTER 9

NAME OPTION #6: USE PROFESSIONAL NAME AND SOCIAL/PERSONAL NAME

Description of Name Option #6

With this option, a person uses one name professionally (often the birth surname) and another name socially (often the married last name). Since both cannot be the person's legal name, one name needs to be selected. The social/personal name is often the legal name and the professional name is not, although the opposite may be true.

Some celebrities have chosen this option. Actress Jessica Biel married Justin Timberlake. She continues to go by Biel professionally, yet her legal last name is Timberlake. When Portia deRossi married Ellen DeGeneres, she legally changed her name to DeGeneres but continues to use deRossi in her professional life.

Benefits of Name Option #6

1. **Fair**

- **Win-win.** It feels fair since no one person has to "give up" their name. A person can use both their birth surname and social/married surname. For many, this feels like the best of all worlds.

2. **Professional Continuity**

- **Not starting over.** It helps with continuity in professional life (networking, past clients, publishing, familiarity, brand) since your surname is not eliminated in the work world after marriage.

- **Credit for past work.** You are less likely to lose the connection with your past work and credits under your birth surname.

- **Others can find you.** It is easier for others to find you professionally if the birth surname is not dropped completely.

3. **Can Keep Private and Public Life Separate**

- **Safety and security.** This option makes it more difficult for the media or unsavory types to find you outside the work setting.

4. **Uses One Family Name**

- **Family unit.** It maintains a family unit since there is legally one family name.

Challenges of Name Option #6

1. **Confusing Logistics**

- **Dual identity.** This option can get logistically confusing (e.g., you may get legal documents or checks to cash written to you using your professional name, people don't know you are the same person, don't know what to call you).

Examples of Name Option #6

(Before marriage) Jane Smith and John Jones
(After marriage) Jane Jones (but uses Smith at work, professionally) and John Jones

(Before marriage) Jason Darnell and Daveed Romain
(After marriage) Jason Romain (but uses Darnell at work, professionally) and Daveed Romain

Reviews of Name Option #6

Positive Reviews
I like that I can keep my work world separate from my private world.

I didn't want to give up all that I have worked for in my career, so I didn't want my name to change. This was a good compromise.

It works for us. Most of our friends still call us by our two different names, which is fine. It is just that legally, we have the same last name. If we ever have kids, it will make it easy for them to have this name as well.

Negative Reviews
Sometimes people don't know what to call me since I have two names.

I have had a few problems with government and legal documents being consistent. I have to remember to always sign those documents with my legal name.

Sometimes it feels like I am straddling two worlds.

Notes on Option #6:

These six married last name options reflect the freedom you have to choose a last name that fits you and your lifestyle. You may even come up with something completely different than what I have listed here. The freedom to choose is a privilege fought for by visionary, and quite frankly, badass women. They were ridiculed, jailed, and spat upon for their stance. These strong women recognized that gender-based restrictions, oppressive laws, and requirements to take someone else's name or their rights would be taken away, was not fair. Thank you, Lucy Stone. Everyone—men or women—have a right to select their own last name. Select. Choose. That is freedom for all.

CHAPTER 10

WHAT ABOUT CHILDREN?

Couples often decide to "go traditional" with their married last names simply because they don't know what to do if they have children. They know they want to feel like a family, a unit bonded together, but may not know there are several ways to achieve that goal. One way to make that connection is through names. Although some ideas were briefly discussed in the previous chapters, let's dive a little deeper into ways couples can pass along their surnames through their children while creating a cohesive family.

There are so many things to consider, and people to appease, when thinking about family names —specifically, children's names. To help make the process more manageable, several couples suggested that last names be determined in two steps:

First, decide what names *work best for you and your partner*. For now, don't think about potential future children (refer to information in previous chapters).

Second, look at what you would do *if children entered the picture*. Each of you answer these questions: What does it mean to have children? Why do you want to have children? Of course, there are many reasons people start a family but pay particular attention to responses concerning legacy, perpetuating the family name, etc. Some couples find they want to carry on just one person's name (often the man's name), while others want to pass along both parents' surnames, so each parent is represented and connected to the child by name.

As we saw in Chapters 4-9 on married last name options, some couples want to have one common family last name to create a feeling of togetherness. One woman shared that she would feel like an outsider if her husband and two boys had a different last name from hers. Another person asked who would carry on the family name if the child didn't have the father's surname? He did not ask who would carry on the mother's family name, or both the mother and father's family names. We have an overemphasis in our culture of passing along the father's family name implying the mother's family name has a lesser value. (Remind me again who goes through labor?)

In contrast, one woman stated that having a common last name with her husband and children did not make a family a family. Her sentiment was one I heard from other interviewees. Families look very different today, and it is not unusual to have different last names or combinations of last names. One common name does not create a Norman Rockwell painting or spawn angelic children any more than preventing family dysfunction.

Another concern with children and names is around medical issues. Couples wonder if their child were taken to a hospital emergency room, would they be able to be with their child if they had different last names? Would having one family name reduce confusion of who is or isn't related? Children's medical records list the parent's names. Additionally, most hospitals have policies that state if a child is brought into the ER and the mother or father have different last names, they are treated like all parents with the same rights.

Some couples have concerns about children and school. They are worried about parent-teacher conferences, perceived challenges picking up their own kids at school if they have different last names, or their child's teacher not knowing their relationship. Parents wanted others to know that "I am Latisha's mother" or "Lyle's father" and not a step-parent or neighbor. The concern is rooted in pride and tribe. However, when I checked with school teachers about this concern, they said it is really no longer a problem. Today, it is not unusual for families to have different last names and still be related by blood. Schools do not discriminate because of this, and most school forms accommodate more than one last name in families.

5 Ways to Handle Children's Names

Picking the right first name for your baby takes time; so should the discussion around the child's surname. Names can be given to children in many interesting and creative configurations. Here are five different ways family surnames are passed along to children.

1. **Only One Parent's Surname is Passed Along in the Child's Name.**

   In some heterosexual marriages, the only surname that is passed along is the father's surname. The mother's surname is not included in the children's first, middle, or last name. Some couples prefer this approach, while others find it unfair and patriarchal.

2. **Child Gets One Parent's Surname as His/Her Middle Name, the Other Parent's Surname as the Last Name**

   Some people are returning to this naming practice that was quite common for many years in the United States and western cultures. It is also a popular option with same-sex couples with children. Typically, each child is given the mother's last name as the child's middle name, and the father's last name is the child's last name (or vice versa). For example, Frank Lloyd

Wright was given his mother's surname as his middle name and his father's surname as his last name. Some people regularly refer to themselves using all three names: first, middle, and last name.

This option ensures that all the children have the same middle and last names, creating a family unit. If both parents choose to keep their birth surnames, this is a great way to honor everyone and connect back to both parents. Lucy Stone's daughter was named Alice Stone Blackwell.

This child naming option continues and honors both parents' names going forward. It is a way to ensure that each parent's lineage does not end. Additionally, when both family surnames are given to a child, it helps future generations track ancestry and family lines.

3. **Child Gets One Parent's Surname as First Name and Other Parent's Surname as the Last Name**
A person's surname can also be passed along through a child's first name. This was a common naming practice in the 1800s in the United States and is still practiced by some in the South. If Elizabeth Washington (née Wiley) had a child, the child's first name would be Wiley. Monica Keller (née Harrison) may give her child the first name of Harrison.

4. **Female Child Gets Mother's Surname, the Male Child Gets Father's Surname**
Another naming option for children is giving a female child the mother's surname and a male child the father's surname. One woman and her husband named their children in this way because "it made sense to us." They felt it was egalitarian and not as patriarchal as the traditional naming process. Although

it does not have a family under one common surname, it does form a family web of interwoven names and connections. As one person said, women who care about passing on their name through the generations would want daughters with their name as much as men want sons with their name.

A small number of states have laws that restrict what surname a child receives. For example, in Tennessee, a child cannot be given a surname that does not include the father's surname unless there is a concurrent submission of a sworn application by both parents.

5. **Hyphenated Last Name for Child that Includes both Parents' Surnames**

    Hyphenating is a way to pass along both the mother's and father's surnames to the child. However, giving a child a hyphenated last name is basically only good for one generation, and then it becomes too long and cumbersome. As mentioned previously, hyphenated names can have challenges with computer forms not accepting the hyphen symbol or the name being too long for the space. Hyphenated surnames can cause confusion requiring spelling. Sometimes, one of the two names in the hyphenated name gets dropped.

    A unique way of hyphenating the parents' names together is putting one parent's last name with the child's first name rather than the last name. For example, the late Congressman and civil rights legend John Lewis was married to Lillian Miles Lewis. They had one son named John-Miles Lewis. The mother's birth surname was hyphenated with their son's first name.

Children's Surnames in Other Cultures

As you can see, there is no universal way to handle children's last names. Here is a sampling of how other cultures name their children.

Up until 2005, France required by law that children take the surname of their father. The French Civil Code now permits parents to give their children either the mother or father's family name or a hyphenation of both. In cases of disagreement, the father's name applies.

Most people in Spanish-speaking countries, such as Spain or Mexico, use two surnames: their father's and their mother's surnames. Children receive the first surname from the father and the second from the mother. However, the parents may choose which surname goes first as long as all their children's names are consistent and in the same order.

In Vietnam, the child can take the mother or the father's surname, although most take the father's surname.

In Chinese culture, the given name is selected by the parents. The name is often found in a dictionary or ancient literary works and includes characters such as beauty, light, hope, talent. It reflects the parents' wish for their child. Children may use either parent's surname, although it is most common to use the father's surname. The surname comes first in the line of names. It is not uncommon for children with the same parent to have different surnames.

In the Arab world, since most women do not take their husbands' last name at marriage, children may be given both the mother and father's surnames as middle and family surnames. However, often the children are given just the father's family surname. Additionally, when a female is born, she is often given her mother's first name, grandmother's first name, and great grandmother's first name (which can be the same name). This is understandable after all; before modern paternal tests existed, a person's lineage was only guaranteed maternally.

Most children get the mother's surname as their middle name and the father's surname as their last name in the Philippines.

Although the mother generally retains her birth surname in South Korea and Taiwan, the children may get the mother's or the father's surname. Just as this book was going to press, South Korea announced the death of 95-year-old Lee Hyo-jae. Ms. Lee was one of South Korea's foremost activists on behalf of women's rights and democracy. She helped abolish the patriarchal naming system, allowing people to use two surnames to reflect their heritage from both parents.

Children in Norway automatically receive the mother's surname unless the parents tell authorities they wish something different.

Parents in the Netherlands can choose their child's surname. If they don't, the father's surname is automatically used for the child. If the couple isn't married, the mother's surname is used for the child.

In Iceland, surnames have a gender-specific suffix (-dóttir = daughter, -son = son).

In Greece, if a man has a daughter and his name is Papadopoulos, she may be named Papadopoulou (that is if the couple decides their children will take his surname). This literally means "the daughter of" a man named Papadopoulos.

In some cultures, especially those with Slavic languages such as Bulgarian, Russian, Slovak, Czech, surnames can change form depending on the gender of the child such as Podwiński/Podwińska in Polish and Nový/Nová in Czech or Slovak. When a daughter comes along, Russian-Slovac tradition adds "ova" to the family name for her. For example, the family name of Sokol would become Sokolova; Mikhail becomes Mikhailova.

That may have been more than you wanted to know about how surnames around the world incorporate gender and marriage status. However, you've got to admit it is kind of interesting. The bottom line is that how we handle children's surnames is not universal. It is based on factors that can change over time and international boundaries. It is up to you what names you want your child to have and if it includes both parents' names.

Reviews about Children's Last Names

My brother, sister, and I all have our mother's maiden name as our middle names and Dad's name as our last name. I love the connection to both sides of the family and to all my siblings.

We have two kids and we all have my husband's last name. The kids have fun first and middle names. I never occurred to me to give them my name at all!

I did not change my last name when I married and our children have their father's last name. My husband even suggested doing a combination of our names but I didn't care. Now I do. Even after 15 years, that decision still haunts me. I wonder how many women are like me, looking at their children and wondering why they carry someone else's name.

If I had it to do over, I would have given my girls my last name, and my son my husband's last name. After all, my genealogical line is as important as his.

Many American women say they change their names for the sake of family cohesion. But look at the world's strongest family-oriented cultures (Italian, Latin American). Women don't delete their last names. There is no confusion about who is a member of the family.

I've had zero problems keeping my maiden name and retaining a tight-knit family with 3 kids. They all have names from both me and my wife.

When my daughter was born, we gave her my last name. We agreed to a matrilineal line for girls in our family, and patrilineal for boys.

I didn't want to give my kids an awkward hyphenated name. So, they got my husband's surname as their last name, and my surname as their middle name. It makes us all feel related and connected.

CHAPTER 11

TIPS FOR TALKING TO YOUR SPOUSE-TO-BE

If you are concerned about your future spouse's reaction to your last name preference, read on. Although you are the best judge of the people in your world, just remember it is human nature to build things up in your mind to be much worse than they really are. The anticipation that your spouse-to-be will react badly may even create a knot in your stomach. Who knew butterflies and knots could co-exist? If you are clear about the last name that works for you and think through how to communicate that to your partner, it will be a less stressful conversation. It will also give you both confidence and comfort with your decision.

Many people have not thought much about married last names, while others have strong ideas and opinions. A 2010 study found that some people perceived women who took their husbands' names a dependent, emotional, and caring, while those women who kept their birth surnames as smart, independent, ambitious, and less caring. These stereotypes, from a study over ten years old, can still smolder as an undercurrent in discussions.

People can also get emotional about names for different reasons. Some may even feel uncomfortable or threatened when a name decision does not fall into their way of thinking. I will say that my husband, like so many others I interviewed, understood why

I wanted to keep my name. He didn't want to change his, so how could he ask me to change mine? If your name preference is concerning to someone else, that may say more about them than you. If that is the case, it will be important to get to the core of this concern and not ignore it.

Now is the time to talk about married names with your spouse-to-be. Some couples talk about names when dating, while others discuss it right after they get engaged. The important thing is not to wait or discuss it the week before the wedding. If your partner refuses to discuss it, I have two words: red flag. If it is important to you, it should be important to him or her. I would be cautious around someone who feels your name and identity is fundamentally worth less than his/her own name. If he praises the virtues of having one family name (e.g., his name) but won't even consider using or incorporating yours...? Red flag, again.

Chances are one person in the couple has thought about names much more than the other person, so it may take some time to get to a common ground and base of understanding. Names can be a big deal for one or both of you, and it may take more than one sit-down discussion to come to a resolution. If you have differing thoughts on the subject, allow time to process both of your concerns and digest new ideas to reach a consensus.

Choose a location for your talk that is quiet, comfortable, and with no interruptions. Select a private spot where no one can overhear the conversation from the next room. This topic is worthy of intimate couple time.

Discussion Points
Add "married last names" to the list of prenuptial issues to discuss before saying "I do." Choosing a last name goes along with pick-

ing a dish pattern, honeymoon location, kids, pets, how to handle money, careers, chores, religion, where to live, how much dust and dirt one can live with, etc.

Like anything, names can bring up deeply held expectations about what marriage should look like based on your own upbringing and family of origin. Consequently, it is important to discuss this topic in a loving and calm manner. Listen to your partner's thoughts and feelings as you would want him or her to listen to yours. Think ahead about what you want to say in the discussion and what your name means to you. Be clear about your feelings.

Sometimes it is helpful to have a prepared sentence or question in your head to jumpstart the conversation. You may want to break the ice with something like: *"I have been thinking a lot about what to do with our names when we get married. I'd love to talk to you about it and get your thoughts."* This shows that you value your partner's opinion and feelings as you do your own. Feel free to bring along notes that might help facilitate communicating your ideas.

Discuss the pros and cons of each name option highlighted in Chapters 4-9 and which option you prefer. Take some of the name options for a spin. Talk about "what if" scenarios and see how that feels to both of you. You may also want to talk to friends who have chosen different name options.

Some additional questions about names to discuss with your partner might include:

- What are your expectations about "our" names after marriage (not just your name)?

- Let's talk about why we each feel that way (get to the root of the feelings, expectations, try to reach the epicenter of your concerns).

- What does your name mean to you?

- What are your fears and concerns about our name choices?

- How can they be addressed or resolved? You may find it useful to refer to the information in the history and culture chapter and use it as a foundation for discussion.

One woman shared that she was worried about what her fiancé would think about last names, specifically his name and family tradition. She thought it would be a hard conversation, but it wasn't. He realized he would not want to change his name so he had empathy for her if she changed her name. Plus, many of their friends had kept their own names.

Reactions from Others

I have to be honest. I was reluctant to devote much space to the topic of others' reactions because I didn't want to give it more ink than it deserved. For the most part, it is a non-issue. By that I mean, few people I talked to experienced pushback from their spouse-to-be or family. Most people don't react negatively about married name choices as they might have in years past. That being said, some brides- and grooms-to-be still worry about how others will respond. I hope this information will help put those concerns to rest and give you the skills to address them if they arise.

Here are a few worst-case scenarios (maybe I should have been an insurance agent) so you will be prepared to handle reactions with confidence.

- **From the family:** As a general courtesy, tell parents and in-laws about your name decision before they hear it from others. Although we all want to be considerate, you should not be swayed by Aunt Ruth or your father-in-law saying, *"it isn't right that you didn't take his name"* or *"you need to change your name to your husband's"* or *"In the Greek tradition in our family, the wife always takes the man's name."*

- **From the spouse-to-be:** Men raised in a more macho or conservative patriarchal environment may say, *"Aren't you proud to be my wife?"* *"What will my friends say?"* *"Nobody will know we are married."*

Negative reactions about your name choice may simply mean your partner or others have a different view of the world and life experience than you do. Many may feel they had to follow "tradition" in their generation (or didn't know there were options), so you should too. They may be unaware of the history, have not given it much thought, are insensitive to your concerns, or simply have strong views about a woman's role.

On the flip side, you may be surprised at the accolades you hear with non-traditional name choices. I heard from several women who kept their birth surnames and were supported by their mothers (who had changed their names). When I told my father about my choice to keep my name when I got married, he looked at me and just smiled. A man of few words and my biggest cheerleader, I could tell in my heart he supported this decision. It wasn't that I kept "his name", he later told me, but rather that I kept my own. I was my own person who was also now married. One identity did not have to disappear for a new one to appear. He proudly introduced my husband and me by our full names. That made *me* smile.

7 Ways to Get Unstuck

What if you reach an impasse after having a conversation with your partner about last names? Here are some tips to try:

- **Identify the problem area.** Where are you getting stuck in the conversation or the decision-making process? Agree on where it is, write it down and revisit it at a later time when you both have had time to think about it (give yourself at least a week). If keeping your birth surname makes your partner feel uneasy, explore where that insecurity is originating. Perhaps you can explore other ways to symbolize your commitment.

- **Perspective.** Present different scenarios regarding how your name choice will work in the real world. This will help your partner more easily visualize and understand your perspective. For example, if she/he thinks it is important for the family to have one name, suggest using your last name rather than her/his. If your suggestion is received with laughter or a resounding "no way!", point out that he/she must now understand how you feel. Or if your partner says, "my family won't be happy" or "my friends will give me a bad time," talk about valuing *your* feelings since you are the one giving up a lot using a new name.

In *The Oregonian* newspaper's "Dear Carolyn" advice column, a man wrote in to say he wanted his wife to take his last name. It was a second marriage for both of them, and she did not want to change her name. Carolyn's response to him was that as someone who had never been asked or pressured to make that core shift, he couldn't fairly ask his fiancé to undertake another name change against her will. *"I feel for you, but her sacrifice outweighs yours."*

- **Do a "feelings check-in."** When you reach an impasse, pause and say you want a feelings check-in. Ask your partner how he/she is feeling at this point. Is either one of you feeling pressured to give in to the other? Discuss what happens when one person gives in (such as building feelings of resentment and anger, feeling undervalued, unheard, etc.).

- **Children.** If children's last names are at the center of the impasse, review the options presented in Chapter 10.

- **Talk to others.** Talk to other couples who have tried the name option that is at the heart of your impasse. How has it worked for them?

  If you can't get beyond an impasse, engage the help of a neutral third party (such as a counselor) to facilitate reaching a solution that works for everyone.

- **Make a decision and review it later**. Lastly, remember that nothing is permanent. If you and your partner want to change your name later, you probably can. However, it is less of a hassle and less expensive for all concerned to change or not change a name at the time of marriage.

CHAPTER 12

Q & A
MONIKER MISCELLANEOUS

Q: What is the Legal Process to Change Last Names?

The easiest time to change a last name in the United States is in conjunction with a marriage or divorce. There are forms you complete at that time that are free or low cost. The form or the marriage license itself asks for the name you will be using from that point forward. Whatever you say you are going to do, do it. This is a legal document. A person can take the official copies of these forms with them to DMV, banks, government offices, etc., to show the name was legally changed due to a marriage or divorce.

It is not unusual for your feelings about your last name to change over time. If you decide later to change your name, it probably can be done. Go to your local county clerk's website or to an attorney to determine the process. Each state has its own requirements for name changes. Some states require public notice and a waiting period, along with an in-person hearing. If your situation is simple and straight-forward, you may be able to download the forms, submit them, and complete the court process yourself for little money. However, if you have legal questions or your situation is complicated, contact an attorney.

Q: Do You Have a Checklist of Places I Need to Notify When I Change My Name?

The following is a list of places to notify if you change your name. You may have other places or entities you need to contact as well. After you change your name, prioritize your notification list, so it feels less overwhelming. Start with the most important places (especially focus on the legal list below) and chip away at the rest of the list. It may take several weeks or months. A name change may feel more complicated than it used to be because of the complexities of life, technology, and security concerns. There are also online businesses that sell name change kits that you might want to explore (be sure and read the reviews before purchasing).

Legal

Social Security
Driver's license
Vehicle(s) registration
Car title
Loan documents
Mortgage (or rental and lease agreements)
All contracts
Passport
Voter registration
Credit cards
Debit cards
Bank accounts, checks
Wills
Trusts
Deeds
IRS
Homeowners' associations
Military (e.g., benefits)

Personal
Utilities (gas, electric, water, cable, sewer, phone, internet)
Insurance (life, auto, home, AAA, etc.)
Personal email address (if it contains your former name)
User names for accounts (if it is your email you are changing)
Investments
Retirement accounts
Financial advisor
Accountant
Lawyer
Doctor's office records
Dentist's office records
School records
Veterinary office records
Pet chip information
Post office boxes
Gym memberships
Portals (e.g., medical, financial, other services)
Magazines (online and mailed)
Voice mail greetings
Social media (e.g., Twitter, Facebook)
Frequent flyer programs
Loyalty programs (e.g., stores)
Membership stores (e.g., Costco)
Alumni associations
Clubs and organizations
Board and volunteer organizations
Address labels for mail
Notifying friends and family of new name and contact info

Work
Human resources (do first)
Paycheck/payroll

Identification (cards, badges)
Voice-mail greeting
Email address (if it includes your former name)
Notifying co-workers of your name change and contact info
Business cards
Resumé
Professional organizations
Credentialing organizations
W2 forms
Unions

Q: What Are the Etiquette Rules for Non-traditional Married Last Names?

The term "etiquette" dates back to France in the 1700s. It may feel old-fashioned, but its purpose can be useful today. Etiquette is simply guidance on protocol, social norms, and common practice, making social situations easier and less stressful. Just as a culture is fluid, so is etiquette. When Emily Post first appeared with her etiquette book in 1922, it was viewed as "the law." Now life is more relaxed and accomodating. Social etiquette around married last names has changed, and it will no doubt change again.

Let's explore ways to handle social situations with the six married last name options.

Announcing Your Name Choice

Wedding websites are common these days as a way to coordinate the event and provide information for guests. These sites inform friends and family about the upcoming wedding, reception, gift registries, and other details. It is also a great place to let others know about your last name plans so everyone is informed. You don't want to end up with engraved wine glasses with the wrong names. There are several ways to word your name announcement on a website or social media: "Seth and Monique will each be keeping their own last names when they marry" or " Both Darias and Ayana will be hyphenating their last names (Drummond-Gilford) when they marry" or "Michelle and Jennifer will be using the family name "Proctor" when they marry."

Introductions

Handling introductions is another area that couples fear will be challenging with different last names or hyphenated names. Don't worry. It is not difficult.

The first introduction you will have as a married person is probably at your wedding. Typically, at the end of the ceremony, the officiant says, *"I now introduce you to Adya and Udarsh Gupta, husband and wife."* If the last names are different, the officiant can say the couple's first names and their new status, *"I now introduce you to Brianna and Amani, wife and husband," "It is my pleasure to introduce the newlyweds, Markham and Thomas", "I now pronounce Riki and Natashia married."* Another option is to state the couple's first and last names and new status, *"I now pronounce Cooper Burgess and Samuel Withers married," "I now introduce you to Zephan Luecke and Lizette Spencer Luecke, husband and wife,"* or *"Let me introduce Palm Spring's newest married couple, Jazin Stenson and Lawanda Jackson."*

How the officiant handles the introduction at the wedding or the DJ at the reception is an often-overlooked detail. Be sure the person doing the introduction knows your name preference.

Basic social introductions at parties or professional gatherings are handled like most introductions, whether or not the couple has different last names. Simply state the relationship and then the name. *"Ansel, I'd like you to meet my wife, Dayna Schmitt."*

Correspondence

What is the etiquette regarding addressing envelopes and other correspondence when a couple has different last names? It is simple. Write both names out in full.

When a married couple's last names differ, both names should be written out on a single line. The envelope should have the two names written out in full and in alphabetical order of the last name. If it is a heterosexual couple, some prefer to put the woman's name first. However, etiquette leans more towards the alphabetical guidance, for example, "Ms. Traci Sanders and Mr. Robert Simon." Inner envelopes that are used with some wedding invitations follow the same rules. However, the first names are not used with the inner envelope. It should be written out as "Ms. Sanders and Mr. Simon." Many people these days simply do not use an honorific.

If one person in a couple dropped their last name and took the partner's last name, correspondence can be handled in several ways. There is the older way, which is going out of favor, as mentioned above (Mr. and Mrs. Edward Solin), or the names may be fully written out such as "Ms. Alicia Randall Solin and Mr. Edward Solin" or "Alicia and Edward Solin." One woman shared that she and her husband were both doctors and shared the same last name. They got mail from time-to-time (incorrectly) addressed to "Dr. and Mrs. Richard Romero." It should be "Drs. Emily and Richard Romero" or "Dr. Emily Romero and Dr. Richard Romero." Either name can go first.

Until recently, women were to be addressed per their marital status on correspondence and in social settings. If a woman was married, the honorific "Mrs." was used at the beginning of her name. After Mrs., the husband's first and last name would be written rather than her name. His name completely subsumed her — her first name as well as her birth surname disappeared. In other words, a woman would be addressed as Mrs. James Fontaine (not Helen Smith or even Helen Fontaine). Today, it is still common to see correspondence addressed to a couple by only using his name, for example "Mr. and Mrs. James Fontaine." If she became widowed or divorced, correspondence could then be addressed a little differently. "Mrs." would still be used but followed by her first name (rather than his), then his last name. For example, Mrs. Helen Fontaine means there was once a man in her life, but now there isn't. Today, even for formal occasions such as wedding invitations, these rules have relaxed. It is now acceptable for both married and divorced women to be referred to by their first names after the title Mrs., as in "Mrs. Fahari Lawson."

One woman who had kept her birth surname said she and her husband would occasionally get correspondence addressed to "Dylan and Sofia" with no last names. A few cards came to "Dylan Mitchell and Family," which was odd because it was just the two of them. They didn't have kids, not even a goldfish. Although they weren't sure what to make of it, they determined most of these oddly addressed envelopes came from the husband's divorced male friends. Their married friends and family got both their first and last names correct.

99.9% of the time, our mail comes to Marcia Morgan and Andy Jordan. However, there is the occasional letter addressed to "The Jordans," the "Morgan-Jordans," "Andy and Marcia Jordan," or plain-old "Andy and Marcia," with no last names. We have never gotten upset by any of these rare variations. We just smile and, when the opportunity arises, let the person know our names. If you are the person writing the envelope and are unsure about each person's name, contact the couple, and find out their names. They will appreciate it. Do not make assumptions these days.

How do you correctly make a last name plural and inclusive of more than one person? Last names are written out in their entirety and never with an apostrophe. When signing or addressing correspondence, write out the last name and add an "s" to the end. However, if the name ends in ch, sh, s, x, or z, add an "es." The Birch family becomes the Birches, Williams becomes Williamses, Rodriquez becomes Rodriguezes. One exception to the rule is if the "x" is silent at the end of the name, in which case you just add an "s" not "es". The Devereaux family becomes the Devereauxs.

Monograms and Other Name-Related Gifts

The monogramming of towels, glasses, silver, notecards, or cloth napkins has long been a wedding gift tradition. Although not as popular as it once was, monogramming is common in many parts of the country.

The word monogram means "one letter." This is because the initials are often overlapping, and to the eye, they look like a single symbol. Monograms began on Greek coins and later became the symbol for royal families. Today something monogrammed is an identifier of a family unit, like a family crest with letters.

But what do you do if the surnames of the couple are not the same? One woman told me to simply marry someone whose surname starts with the same letter as your surname. Okay, if that is not an option, etiquette experts suggest:

- A couple's monograms do not need to be identical. A common towel color and common embroidery thread color on the lettering is often used to look like a set. As an added benefit, it is a great way to avoid getting each other's towels mixed up!

- Some people blend the couple's initials into one monogram. For example, each spouse's last name initial is combined into a graphic design or shape.

- The last name initial is always in the middle, first name initial on the left, middle name initial on the right.

- The monograms can be all the same height, or the last name initial in the center can be enlarged.

- If a person kept his/her birth surname as a middle name (Sailor) and added the spouse's last name (Thomas) at the end (Linda Sailor Thomas), the last name would be a large T in the middle of the monogram with the other letters small on each side. LTS

- If a person kept his/her birth surname and did not add their spouse's surname to the end of their name (as an example, Linda Ann Sailor), the monogram would be LSA.

Q: Should I Change My Name After Divorce?

In the United States, approximately 50% of marriages end in divorce (I guess we should be glad we aren't in Russia with a 65% divorce rate or Cuba with 70%). There can be challenges when a marriage breaks up, including emotional baggage around last names. If you changed your surname when you got married, you would be carrying your former spouse's name even though you may not want anything to do with the old marriage or his/her family. Does the person who gave up his/her surname hang onto the ex-spouse's last name forever, possibly bringing up bad memories, associations, and feelings?

After divorce, a person does not automatically revert to their birth surname. A divorce decree must specifically state the future name you intend to use, and the decree be signed by the parties. However, some people go back to their birth surname when a marriage ends, and the whole "changing records" process begins again. The decision can be complicated if you have used your married last name as an adult for many years and have built contacts and a reputation in personal and professional settings. Your children may also share that last name. Simply reverting to your birth surname may not feel like a good fit at this point in adulthood.

Cheryl Strayed (née: Nyland), author of *Wild*, created a new last name for herself after her divorce. She felt it was symbolic and a way to take full responsibility for her new life. She liked the wanderlust feeling she got from the name Strayed.

Many people, after a divorce, are ready to move on. One way to do that is by shedding the shared name with the former spouse. Other women felt like it was their name now and claimed it.

Some women said that their former husbands had remarried, some more than once, and that there were now several "Mrs. His Name" out there in the world (the wives had all changed their names to his). This situation not only caused confusion but some resentment by the women. If you kept your birth surname when you married or went back to it after a divorce, confusion with your partner's former or future spouse(s) is eliminated.

What about a second marriage or beyond? Does the person keep changing his/her name with each marriage? If you remarry at some point and still have your former spouse's name as your own, do you change your name *again*? If you change it and have children from the first marriage, they may now have a different last name than you (e.g., their father's name). If you keep your first husband's last name in the new marriage, what are the feelings associated with carrying the previous spouse's name? If you change your name to the new spouse's name, you are starting all over again (work reputation, friends, forms, records, accounts, etc.). Many women find that this is a good time to go back to their birth surname and keep it. Forever.

All of this reminds me of an old *Saturday Night Live* skit about actress Susan Lucci who starred in the daytime television show "*All My Children.*" Her character had been married nine times (actually 10 times, one man twice), and each time she changed her last name. The skit revolved around calling her by all nine last names each time she was addressed.

One woman shared that she had changed her surname when she got married and kept that surname after divorcing. When she remarried, she kept my first husband's surname since she was well into adulthood and career. It was fine with her new husband but caused quite an outcry from some friends and family.

Another woman stated that when she married a man with children, she kept her name because it was her identity, her family's legacy, plus her new husband's first wife already had his name. She did not want to "start over" in her profession with a new name, and she did not like the sound of his last name with her first name. For her, she said, it was an easy decision.

University of Florida professor Diana Boxer found that most women who have children and then divorce do *not* go back to using their birth surnames because they want to continue to share the same last name with their children. However, she found that many women who remarry do not hesitate to change to their new husband's last name even though now their name would be different from their children's last name.

Another woman shared that she was divorced with two daughters. She kept her ex-husband's last name because she didn't want to have a different last name from her children. Within six years, the daughters were married and had all changed their names, like she had done when she got married. She said that unfortunately, she was now stuck being the only one with her ex-husband's name! She stated that she realizes that the love for her kids would not have been less if she had gone back to her birth surname after the divorce (she could have also changed her last name after her children were grown). It reminds me of people I have known who moved to another city to be closer to their adult children, only to find after a few years their children moved away because of jobs, etc. You need to decide for yourself since others are also making decisions for themselves.

Here is what some people said about names and divorce:

When I got a divorce, I was very glad I had kept my maiden name. I didn't have to go through the trouble of changing my name back.

We attended a wedding where the bride's parents had divorced and her father had remarried. The invitation read: "Mrs. Marcus Jackson" and on the next line, "Mr. and Mrs. Marcus Jackson", and the next line said "request the honor of your presence at the wedding of their daughter April Ann to Robert Ralston." Even when divorced, the mother of the bride referred to herself as the wife of her ex-husband. It seemed very bizarre - the women had no names!

When I married a second time, once again, I changed my surname to my husband's. Essentially, I wanted to rid myself of my first husband's name. I should have reverted to my maiden name or never changed it to begin with.

When I married, I was so proud to be a "Mrs." I immediately had notecards printed and a custom doormat made. After divorcing, I reclaimed my maiden name. My divorced sister did the same. When our father died, his obituary listed us with our maiden names. Our mother was so embarrassed because she thought people would think neither of us were able to land a husband!

When I got married, I felt hopeful, proud and apprehensive all at the same time about my new identity. Nineteen years later after my divorce, I returned to the name I was born with. I am not giving up that name again.

I eagerly returned to my maiden name when I divorced and kept it in my second marriage. I am proud of my name which is easier to spell and pronounce than either husbands' names.

When I got divorced, I kept his last name because it seemed easier to do. The other reason was he didn't want me to keep it and spite seemed like as good a reason as any to hang onto it.

A co-worker who was getting divorced had to have her name change published in local newspapers. She was so embarrassed and mad that her husband didn't have to go through that experience like she did.

My friend Mary in Minnesota wrote a poem after getting a divorce summing up her feelings about her name:

> *But my attitude's different now,*
> *I've changed and I've grown.*
> *I need that freedom that once I had known.*
> *I want a symbol to announce my rebirth.*
> *I want my own name back, and I want my own worth.*

CHAPTER 13

"CHOOSING YOUR MARRIED LAST NAME" GUIDED WORKSHEET

Now that you've read through the history of marriage and names, as well as the six name options and reviews, what do you think? Has a clear last name choice emerged for you and your partner? If so, great!

If not, here are a few exercises to help you narrow things down a bit and decide on a name. If you are like me, you overthink things. But for this exercise, just write down your *gut* reaction. Write fast without self-judgment or edits. In other words, jot down what pops into your mind.

1. **List how you feel right now about your current last name (list the feelings).**

Now, go back and circle the feelings that are the *most* important to you.

2. **If you could keep your last name in some form after mar-
    riage (e.g., retain last name, use as middle name, hyphen-
    ate), how would you feel? (list the feelings)**

Now, go back and circle the feelings that are the *most* important
to you.

3. **If you no longer had your last name in any form, how would
    you feel? (list the feelings)**

Now, go back and circle the feelings that are the *most* important
to you.

4. **This book presents the benefits and challenges of each name
    option. At this point, chances are you're leaning towards one
    or two of the options. With that in mind, look back at your
    responses to questions 1-3 and the feelings you listed. What
    feelings do you want to experience, and with which option
    are they associated? Pay particular attention to the things
    you circled. They are your priorities. Now make a decision!**

First name choice:

Second name choice:

Third name choice:

5. **Try it out!** Your homework assignment this week is to live with your first choice for a married last name. Pretend you are now married and using that name. (a) Visualize going to the grocery store or gym. Imagine the clerk or staff calling you by that name and *hearing* that name. (b) You are at a social gathering, and you are introduced with that name. You introduce yourself to others *using* that name. (c) If you fill out a form or get mail, imagine *seeing* that name on paper.

    If your spouse is also changing his/her name, have them do these same exercises. At the end of the week, sit down with your spouse-to-be and discuss your *feelings* and experiences with your top choice. Most people get clarity from this exercise. If not, try out your second choice for a week and so on. Jot down some notes during the week as you go through this exercise.

ACKNOWLEDGMENTS

The ocean inspires and feeds me. Its vastness opens my mind to possibilities, and the salty breeze makes me want to soar with joy like a seagull with a French fry. I crave those feelings when I hunker down and write. My dear friends Dave and Anne O'Brien were gracious in letting me use their beach house for a writing retreat. I spent time by myself scribbling notes on large easel paper and taping them to the walls—the smell of magic markers wafting in the air. The vacation home looked more like a war room, yet no enemy was advancing: just ideas.

Another writing retreat took me to a grand old log house at the coast owned by the Oregon Writer's Colony. Each carved log, stacked and orderly, had a rich history of witnessing stories written within its walls. The black soot on the imposing stone fireplace told a tale of crumpled pages with discarded writers' words. When you are alone for days on end, a monkish silent retreat, you notice these things. In fact, maybe you notice too much, and your imagination hyperventilates. During the day, I was contemplative, as I wrote. Each keystroke had the grace of a slow dance, where you lock eyes with your partner, feeling each gentle move and waiting for it to lead you to the next step. But the evenings were quite a different story. I wrote briskly to get all the words on the page before, you know, something happened. Darn, I wish I had not watched *The Shining*. I waited for Jack Nicolson to break through the door with an ax at any moment. But I have to say, these two writing approaches worked together in an odd sort of marriage. At least I got a lot of writing done.

Thank you to the amazing, trail-blazing academics and researchers in the field of gender, family, onomastics, and linguistics. Their studies and perspectives were highlighted throughout the book: Diana Boxer, Professor of Linguistics, University of Florida; Laurie Scheuble, Emeritus - Sociology, Pennsylvania State University; Jane Eisner, Philadelphia Inquirer, Forward; Brian Powell, Professor of Family and Gender, Indiana University-Bloomington; Richard Coates, Professor Emeritus of Onomastics, Bristol Centre for Linguistics, University of the West of England; Elizabeth Aura McClintock, Professor, University of Notre Dame. Thank you to Igor Krupnik, Chair, Department of Anthropology, Smithsonian - National Museum of Natural History, and JoAllyn Archambault, Ethnologist and former head of the Department's Native American Program, Smithsonian - National Museum of Natural History, for their research assistance.

Thank you to my sister, Dana Morgan McBrien, for supporting my ideas and projects through the years. She read the early draft of my book, offering different perspectives and constructive sisterly feedback. As an ordained minister who has officiated many weddings (including my own), her experience enriched her critique. Thank you to Deborah Bouchette and Laura Chase, Oregon Writers Colony, who volunteered their time to read the beta draft, which is not always an easy or pretty task. They offered great suggestions to make the book better.

A huge thank you to Ellen Waterston, author, poet, and founder of the Writers' Ranch (www.writingranch.com) for reading a draft and offering her rich insights and experience. She is an amazing writer, teacher, and overall inspiring person.

Thank you to my "M Salon" women friends: Martha, Mimi, Molly, Marie, Merritt, Mogul (aka Susan), Moon (aka Linda), and Monkey (aka Patsy). They are my cheering section. Their energy, laughter, Zoom happy hours, and encouragement kept me going throughout the pandemic and while slogging through the writing and research.

A heartfelt thank you goes to the many women and men who allowed me to interview them for the book. They shared personal thoughts and feelings, intimate conversations, and deeply-held beliefs, illuminating the struggles around changing a last name. The candor about their own upbringing, their parent's marriages, as well as their own, brought insight and a real-life perspective to the book. Their voices reflect the shifting culture and role of gender in marriage.

And then there is Andy Jordan. He popped into my life with humor and calm. He listened to my stories and shared his own. When we met, we both had globetrotting happy feet, a condition that lead us on some amazing adventures. His good looks made me wonder if he was the lovechild of Kevin Costner and Mark Harmon on *NCIS*. Our life paths were different, yet somehow, we ended up in the same place in our lives at that moment of meeting. Even as a writer, I struggle to find the words to adequately thank Andy, my husband. We have learned to be together while being ourselves. Thank you, Andy, from the depths of my heart.

As I write this book, we are in the middle of the COVID-19 pandemic. It looks like a vaccine will be coming soon, and the sadness, fear, and suffering will end. By the time you sit down to read the book, the world will look a little different than it does today. But at this very moment, I would be remiss if I didn't share that I am full of gratitude sitting here in the safety of our home. It has become our refuge and haven. As such, I have tried to focus on the resiliency and silver-linings of this moment. The pandemic has afforded me the time to write. I know it is a privilege. I will always be humbled and grateful for this gift.

REFERENCES

Allgor, C. (2012) "Coverture: The Word You Probably Don't Know but Should." *National Women's History Museum.*

Almack, K. (2005) "What's in a Name? The Significance of the Choice of Surnames Given to Children Born within Lesbian Parent Families." *Sexualities.* Vol. 8, pp 239-254

Anthony, D. J. (2010-2011) "A Spouse by Any Other Name." *William and Mary, Journal of Race, Gender and Social Justice.* Vol. 17, Issue 1.

BBC. (November 1, 2014) "Why Should Women Change Their Names on Getting Married?" *BBC News Magazine.*

Berman, J. (December 27, 2017) "Why so Many Women Still Take their Husband's Last Name." *Marketwatch.*

Bindley, K. (October 15, 2011) "Should Women Change Their Last Names After Marriage?" *Huffington Post.*

Boguhn, A. (January 30, 2015) "5 Alternative to Taking Your Spouse's Last Name." *Everyday Feminism Magazine.*

Boxer, D. (June 13, 2006) *American Women, Changing their Names.* All things Considered, National Public Radio interview.

Boxer, D., Gritsenko, E. (2005) "Women and Surnames Across Cultures: Reconstituting Identity in Marriage." *Women and Language,* Vol. 28, pp 1-11

Brides. (2016) "The 6 Major Issues Brides had When Changing Their Names." *Brides Magazine.* August 16, 2016 issue.

Calloway, N. (2020) "Changing Your Name When you Get Married." *The Spruce.*

Carli, L.L. (1999) "Gender, Interpersonal Power and Social Influence." *Journal of Social Issues*. Vol. 55, pp 81-99

Chambers, V., Padnani, A., Burgess, A. (May 15, 2020*)* "The Mrs. Files" *The New York Times*.

Chemaly, S. (July 16, 2015) "It Doesn't Matter if Women Change Their Names When they Marry, It Matters if Men Do." *Role Reboot*.

Chen, Z., Fiske, S.T., Lee, T.L. (2009) "Ambivalent Sexism and Power-Related Gender-Role Ideology in Marriage." *Sex Roles*. Vol. 60, pp 765-778

Clarke, V., Burns, M., Burgoyne, C. (2008) "Who Would Take Whose Name? Accounts of Naming Practices in Same-Sex Relationships." *Journal of Community and Applied Social Psychology*. Vol. 18, pp 420-439

Coontz, S. (2005) *Marriage: A History: From Obedience to Intimacy or How Love Conquered Marriage*. Viking/Penguin Books. New York.

Crooke, J. (September 14, 2019) "Why are Millennial Women Opting Out of Taking Their Husband's Last Name?" *The Christian Post*.

Darrisaw, M. (2018) "16 Common Wedding Traditions and the Shocking History Behind Them." *Southern Living Magazine*. Retrieved from https://www.SouthernLiving.com/weddings/history-weddings-traditions

Emens, E.F. (2007) "Changing Name Changing: Framing Rules and the Future of Marital Names." *The University of Chicago Law Review*. Vol. 74, pp 761-863

Etaugh, C.E., Bridges, J.S., Cummings-Hill, M., Cohen, J. (1999) "Names can Never Hurt Me? The Effects of Surname Use on Perceptions of Married Women." *Psychology of Women Quarterly*. Vol. 23, pp 819-823

Femlee, D. H. (1994) "Who's on Top? Power in Romantic Relationships." *Sex Roles*. Vol. 31, pp 275-295

Finch, J. (2008) "Naming Names: Kinship, Individuality and Personal Names." *Sociology.* Vol. 42, pp 709-725

Filipovic, J. (March 7, 2013) "Why Should Married Women Change Their Name? Let Men Change Theirs." *The Guardian.*

Fleming, J. (September 12, 2013) "Name Change in Marriage Cultural Tradition." *Florala.* https://florala.net/life/name-change-in-marriage-cultural-tradition/article_e142f-b1c-1b0a-11e3-98d8-0019bb30f31a.html

Folger, J. (2019) "Is Keeping Your 'Maiden' Name a Good Financial Move?" *Investopedia.*

Foss, K. A. & Edson, B.A. (1989) "What's in a Name? Accounts of Married Women Name Choices." *Western Journal of Speech Communication.* Vol. 53, pp 356-373

Forbes, G.B., Adams-Curtis, L. E., White, K. B., Hamm, N.R. (2002) "Perceptions of Married Women and Married Men with Hyphenated Surnames." *Sex Roles.* Vol. 46, pp 167-175

Frank, G. (June 28, 2017) "What to Expect When You Don't Change Your Last Name After Marriage: 9 Things to Know." *The Today Show*, NBC.

Gill, K.E. (2014) "My Name is the Symbol of My Identity." *Medium. com* Retrieved from https://medium.com/@kegill/my-name-is-the-symbol-of-my-identity-19f183fd2711

Goldenberg Jones, L. (July 24, 2013) "Should You Change Your Name After Marriage?" *Women Getting Married.* Retrieved from https://womangettingmarried.com/category/wedding-planning-tools/

Goldin, C., Shim, M. (2004) "Making a Name: Women's Surnames at Marriage and Beyond." *Journal of Economic Perspectives.* Vol. 18, pp 143-160

Goldschneider, J. (August 2019) "I Happily Changed My Last Name After I got Married, and 13 Years Later I'm Full of Regret." *Good Housekeeping.*

Gooding, G. E., Kreider, R.M. (2009) "Women's Marital Naming Choices in a Nationally Representative Sample." *Journal of Family Issues.* Vol 31, pp 681-701

Graham, D.A. (November 11, 2015) "A Short History of Hillary (Rodham) (Clinton)'s Changing Names: How the Democratic Candidate's Evolving Self-Identification Tells a Story of Women in American Politics." *The Atlantic.* Retrieved from http:// the atlantic.com/politics/archive/2015/11/a-short-history-of-hillary-rodham-clintons-name/418029/

Hamilton, L., Geist, C. Powell, B. (2011) "Marital Name Change as a Window into Gender Attitudes." *Gender and Society.* Vol. 25, pp 145-175

Hampson, S. (Sept 2007) "Get Hitched – But Keep Your Name." *The Globe and Mail.*

Hampson, S. (Sept 2007) "Give Your Children Mom's Last Name? Don't Mess with Tradition." *The Globe and Mail.*

Hepworth, A. (2020) "5 Real Women on Why they Gave Their Children Their Last Name." *Pure Wow*, Gallery Media Group.

Hilmantel, R. (August 12, 2013) "Why Women Choose to Keep Their Last Names – or Not." *Women's Health.*

Hoffnung, M. (2006) "What's in a Name? Marital Name Choice Revisited." *Sex Roles.* Vol. 55, pp 817-825

Hoffnung, M., Williams, M. (2016) "When Mr. Right Becomes Mr. Wrong: Women's Post-divorce Surname Choice." *Journal of Divorce & Remarriage.* Vol. 57, pp 12-35

Johnson, D. R., Scheuble, L.K. (1995) "Women's Marital Naming in Two Generations: A National Study." *Journal of Marriage and Family.* Vol. 57, pp 724-732

Johnson, D.R., Scheuble, L. K. (2002) "What Should We Call Our Kids? Choosing Children's Surnames when Parent's Last Names Differ." *The Social Science Journal.* Vol. 39, pp 419-429

Kennedy, S. (February 27, 2000) "Why I Changed My Name After My Divorce." *Scary Mommy Blog.*

Kitchener, C. (June 20, 2020) "The Tradition of Taking a Man's Last Name is 'Unquestionably Sexist.' This New Trend Could be the Solution." *The Washington Post.*

Kopelman, R.E., Shea-Van Fossen, R. J., Paraskevas, E., Lawter, L., Protta, D.J. (2009) "The Bride is Keeping Her Name: A 35 Year Retrospective Analysis of Trends and Correlates." *Social Behaviour and Personality.* Vol. 37, pp 687-700

Krebs, C. (2017) "5 Lessons I Learned While Changing My Last Name." *Weddingwire.*

Lockwood, P., Burton, C., Boersma, K. (2011) "Tampering with Tradition: Rationales Concerning Women's Married Names and Children's Surnames." *Sex Roles.* Vol. 65, pp 827-839

MacDougall, P. B. (1985) "The Right of Women to Name Their Children." *Law and Inequity.* Vol. 3, pp 91-159

Mackey, J. (January 23, 2017) "After We're Married, Can My Husband Take My Last Name?" *Brides Magazine.*

Mackey, J. (June 13, 2017) "How to Change Your Name After the Wedding." *Brides Magazine.*

Marriage.Com (2019) "Changing Your Name After Divorce." *Marriage.com* website. https://marriage.com/advice/name-change/changing-your-name-after-divorce

MacEacheron, M. (2016) "North American Women's Marital Surname Change: Practices, Law and Patrilineal Descent Reckoning." *Evolutionary Psychological Science.* Vol. 2, pp 149-161

McClintock, E.A. (2018) "Should Marriage Still Involve Changing a Woman's Name?" *Psychology Today.* Online, September 6, 2018.

Mills, S. (2003) "Caught Between Sexism, Anti-Sexism and Political Correctness: Feminist Women's Negotiations with Naming Practices." *Discourse & Society.* Vol. 14, pp 87-100

Mitchell, E. (January 3, 2017) "Why These 7 Brides Decided to Keep Their Last Name." *Brides Magazine.*

Mitchell, E. (January 19, 2017) "7 Reasons You Might Want to Take His Last Name." *Brides Magazine.*

Ngo, D., (2015) "10 Pros and Cons of Changing Your Name After Marriage." *Your Tango* website. Retrieved from https://www.yourtango.com/201064084/10-pros-and-cons-changing-name-marriage.

Noak, T., Wiik, K. A. (2008) "Women's Choice of Surname upon Marriage in Norway." *Journal of Marriage and Family.* Vol. 70, pp 507-518

Nugent, C. (2010) "Children's Surnames, Moral Dilemmas: Accounting for the Predominance of Father's Surnames for Children." *Gender and Society.* Vol. 24, pp 499-525

Ortberg, D. M. (2019) "Help! My Ex-wife Changed her First Name to my Fiancée's Name." *Slate.*

Pilcher, J. (2017) "Names and 'Doing Gender': How Forenames and Surnames Contribute to Gender Identities, Difference and Inequalities." *Sex Roles.* Vol. 77, pp 812-822

Pilcher, J. (2011) "His, Not Hers: Surnames and Marriage." *June Pilcher Blog.*

Purmont, N.M. (2016) "Do You Change Your Married Name when Your Husband Dies?" *Elle Magazine.* September Issue.

Rainey, S. (July 11, 2013) "More British Women are Keeping Their Last Names after Marriage." *The Telegraph.*

Rapacon, S. (August 2013) "5 Choices for Changing Your Name After Marriage." *Kiplinger's.*

Robnett, R., Wertheimer, M. Tenenbaum, H.R. (2018) "Does a Woman's Marital Surname Choice Influence Perceptions of Her Husband? An Analysis Focusing on Gender-Typed Traits and Relationship Power Dynamics." *Sex Roles.* Vol. 79 (Issue 1-2), pp 59-71

Robnett, R., Underwood, C., Nelson, P., Anderson, K. (2016) "She Might be Afraid of Commitment: Perceptions of Women Who Retain Their Surname After Marriage." *Sex Roles.* Vol. 75 (Issue 9-10), pp 500-513

Ryan, E.G. (November 4, 2011) "Why are We Still Taking our Husband's Last Names?" *The Today Show*, NBC.

Saad, G. (2010) "Do Contemporary American Women Take Their Husband's Surnames?" *Psychology Today*. Online November 21, 2010.

Salie, F. (November 5, 2009) "Change your Name After Marriage – Why?" *Oprah.com*

www.cnn.com/2009/LIVING/wayoflife/11/05/o.change.name.after.marriage/index.html

Scheuble, L. K., Johnson, D.R., Johnson, K. M. (2012) "Marital Name Changing Attitudes and Plans of College Students: Comparing Change over Time and Across Regions." *Sex Roles*. Vol. 66, pp 282-292.

Seattle Bride. (Spring/Summer 2019) "The History Behind Maiden vs. Married Names." *Seattle Bride Magazine.*

Shafer, E. F. (2017) "Hillary Rodham Versus Hillary Clinton: Consequences of Surname Choice in Marriage." *Gender Issues*. Vol. 34, pp 316-332

Simonian, J. (May 2, 2017) "I Kept my Maiden Name and It was a Huge Mistake." Retrieved from [Mom.me] http://msn.com/en-us/lifestyle/family-relationships/i-kept-my-maiden-name-and-it-was

Spencer, M.E. (1973) "A Woman's Right to Her Name." *UCLA Law Review*. Vol. 21, No. 2, pp 665-690

Smith, N. (June 18, 2018) "7 Reasons I Wish I Hadn't Taken my Husband's Last Name." *POPSUGAR*. https://www.popsugar.com/love/reasons-keep-your-surname-43492273

Stannard, U. (1977) *Mrs. Man*. Germain Books. San Francisco, CA.

Tate, D. (2020) "Changing Your Last Name: How to Decide What is Right for You." *The Bridal Guide*. https://www.bridalguide.com/planning/married-life/changing-your-last-name-options

Tate, D. (January 16, 2013) "What's in a (Maiden) Name?" Retrieved from https://mom.me/lifestyle/5422-whats-maiden-name/

Teal, W. (2017) "5 Reasons to Create your Own Last Name After Marriage." *Weddingwire.*

The Feminist Bride. (August 12, 2011) "Why Women Change Their Last Names After Marriage." *The Feminist Bride.*

Thwaites, R. (2013) "The Making of Selfhood: Naming Decisions on Marriage." *Families, Relationships, and Societies.* Vol. 2, pp 425-439

Tigar, L. (2017) "5 Women Reveal Why They Did – or Didn't – Change Their Last Name." *Weddingwire.*

Twenge, J. M. (1997) "Mrs. His Name. Women's Preference for Married Names." *Psychology of Women Quarterly.* Vol. 21, pp 417-429

University of Oregon, Center for the Study of Women in Society. Jane Grant Papers. csws.uoregon.edu/about/jane-grant

Vaidyanathan, R. (June 11, 2015) "A New Wedding Trend? The Men Taking their Wives' Names." *BBC News.* Retrieved from http://www.bbc.co.uk/news/magazine

Valetas, M.F. (2001) "The Surname of Married Women in the European Union." *Population and Societies.* Vol. 367, pp 1-4

Waxman, O.B. (2019) "'Lucy Stone, If you Please': The Unsung Suffragist who Fought for Women to Keep Their Maiden Names." *Time Magazine.* March 7, 2019.

Weiss, S. (June 1, 2016) "Should You Change Your Last Name When You Get Married? Here's How 9 Women Decided." *Huffington Post.*

Williams, V. (Aug 24, 2016) "What's in a Name? For Anne Holton, A Lot of History and the Potential to Make More." *The Washington Post.*

Same-Sex Marriages

Birdwell-Branson, J. "Name Changing Options for Same-Sex Couples After Marriage." *The Wedding Bee.* www.weddingbee.com/category/advice/

Garcia, P. (July 30, 2015) "In a Same-Sex Marriage, Who Gets to Keep Their Name?" *Vogue Magazine.*

Legal Match. (2019) "What is the Law for Name Changes After a Same-Sex Marriage?" *Legal Match* website. https://www.legal-match.com/law-library/article/name-changes-after-same-sex-marriage

The Knot. (2019) "An LGBTQ+ Couple's Guide to Marriage Name Changes." *The Knot* online website. Retrieved from https://www.theknot.com/content/same-sex-marriage-name-change

WHAT DID YOU DECIDE TO DO WITH YOUR SURNAME?

I'd love to hear from you about your last name choice and what you thought about the book. Please visit my website www.marciakmorgan.com and drop me a note. It would be great to connect!

REVIEWS

I'm trying to reach as many people as possible who are about to get married. Can you help me out? The best way to make the book more visible to others is to rate and review it online where it was purchased. If you found the book useful, please take a minute right now to leave a review.

Also, check out my YouTube Channel (Marcia Morgan) for more content, "like" the videos, and share them with others. https://m.youtube.com/channel/UCH6Azefr-1TiWwj8X200zRg

MAKE A DIFFERENCE FOR SOMEONE GETTING MARRIED

After your big day, consider donating your wedding dress to *Brides Across America*. They provide free wedding dresses to military and first responders to ease the financial and planning burden. A giveaway event is hosted twice a year across the country at participating bridal salons. Donations are tax-deductible. www.bridesacrossamerica.com

Wish Upon A Wedding is a nonprofit organization that grants weddings and vow renewals for couples facing serious illness or life-altering circumstances. Ceremonies are completely free to the couple through donations of money, professional services, tuxedos, and bridal dresses. Donations are tax-deductible. www. wishuponawedding.org

FOR PRESENTATIONS AND MEDIA INTERVIEWS

Marcia K. Morgan, Ph.D.
marcia@migima.com
541.389.4098

ABOUT THE AUTHOR

 Marcia K. Morgan, Ph.D., brings a wealth of experience helping to give women and girls a voice. She draws on more than forty years as a national consultant, researcher, and trainer. Morgan has consulted with the US Department of Justice, the Pentagon and was selected to represent the United States in Italy at the NATO conference on victimization. She has appeared on numerous television, radio, and podcast programs.

In 1976, Morgan and a colleague developed the ground-breaking, anatomically-correct dolls now used worldwide to interview victims of child sexual abuse. She initially made her mark heading up one of the first all-female law enforcement rape investigations programs in the US. As Executive Director of Migima, LLC since 1980, Marcia oversees an innovative firm that provides high-energy consulting services in criminal justice and social issues.

Morgan is an author of numerous books and articles, translated into multiple languages, on gender and crime. She is excited to look at gender from a different perspective in this book: marriage and surnames.

Marcia and her husband live in Bend, Oregon.

OTHER BOOKS BY
MARCIA K. MORGAN

GO! How to Get Going and Achieve Your Goals and Dreams at Any Age (a book for women)

SafeTOUCH

How to Interview Sexual Abuse Victims

Interviewing Sexual Abuse Victims Using Anatomical Dolls

My Feelings

Investigating Allegations of Staff Sexual Misconduct with Offenders

Operational Practices in Women's Prisons

Critical Issues in Managing Women Offenders – A Policy Perspective

Women Offenders: Developing an Agency-wide Approach

How to be More Effective Supervising Women Offenders in the Community

Addressing Staff Sexual Misconduct with Offenders

Gender-Responsive Standards and Assessment Tool (G-SAT)

Made in United States
North Haven, CT
24 January 2022

15188738R00114